THE PAMPHLET DEBATE ON THE UNION BETWEEN GREAT BRITAIN AND IRELAND, 1797-1800

(Ed.) *A Festschrift for Francis Stuart on his Seventieth Birthday*
(Dolmen Press, 1972)

Sheridan Le Fanu and Victorian Ireland
(Clarendon Press, 1980; 2nd, enlarged edition Lilliput Press, 1991)

(Ed. with A.J. Stead) *James Joyce and Modern Literature*
(Routledge and Kegan Paul, 1982)

Ascendancy and Tradition
in Anglo-Irish Literary History from 1789 to 1939
(Clarendon Press, 1985)

The Battle of the Books: Two Decades of Irish Cultural Debate
(Lilliput Press, 1987)

(Ed.) Austin Clarke *Selected Poems*
(Penguin Classics, 1992)

Dissolute Characters: Irish Literary History
through Balzac, Le Fanu, Yeats and Bowen
(Manchester University Press, 1993)

The Dublin Paper War of 1786–1788:
a Bibliographical and Critical Inquiry
(Irish Academic Press, 1993)

From Burke to Beckett: Ascendancy,
Tradition and Betrayal in Literary History
(Cork University Press, 1994)

THE PAMPHLET DEBATE ON THE UNION BETWEEN GREAT BRITAIN AND IRELAND, 1797-1800

W. J. Mc CORMACK

> Blare no more ramsblares, oddmund
> barkes! And cease your fumings,
> kindalled bushies! And sherrigoldies
> yeassymgnays; your wildeshaweshowe
> moves swiftly sterneward! For here
> the holy language. Soons to come.
> To pausse.
> *Finnegans Wake* 256.11–15

IRISH ACADEMIC PRESS

Set in 11 on 12 point Ehrhardt
by Koinonia Ltd., Manchester, for
IRISH ACADEMIC PRESS LTD
Kill Lane, Blackrock, Co. Dublin, Ireland
and in North America by
IRISH ACADEMIC PRESS LTD
c/o ISBS, 5804 NE Hassalo Street, Portland, OR 97213

A catalogue entry for this book
is available from the British Library.

ISBN 0-7165-2568-2

Printed in Great Britain
by Antony Rowe Ltd, Chippenham, Wilts

CONTENTS

CONTENTS

PAMPHLETS AND THEIR PROBLEMS

I. THE IRISH PAPER WARS

At first glance, the present book looks very similar to its predecessor, *The Dublin Paper War of 1786-1788* (1993).[1] Both revolve round alphabetically arranged title-lists of pamphlets debating an important Irish political event; both effectively establish that the number of pamphlets published on each occasion was far greater than historians had supposed; and both also demonstrate that the printing and distribution of a single title was a complex business, often involving multiple issues and sometimes even more than one publisher/bookseller. The present book, therefore, could be read as extending our knowledge of late eighteenth-century Irish controversy.

In fact, the two works differ radically with respect both to design and intention. *The Dublin Paper War* employed its check-list to a specific end – that of clarifying the ideological issues at stake in controversies of the mid-1780s. From the outset, the central pamphlet of the 'war' was known; the task in hand was to demonstrate its relationship with changes in the conceptualisation of Irish politics, changes which were thought to have occurred at that time but which proved actual only in the years following 1789. Thus the book contained much more than a list of pamphlets; it advanced a number of related arguments about the Church of Ireland, inter-church relations, tithes, whiteboyism, etc, not to mention a critique of some recent historical work in this area. The list of pamphlets, duly numbered, may (with luck) be taken as complete or, at worst, vulnerable only to minor revisions and additions.

The present list comes pretty well ungarnished. Its components have only been numbered in a preliminary fashion, under the initial letters of their titles, rather than in a cumulative way suggesting some final or total listing. The contents are not analysed either in relation to the use of significant terms or concepts – for example, liberty, the nation, kingdom, emancipation, union etc – nor for their general account of political disputation in the years between 1797

[1] W. J. Mc Cormack, *The Dublin Paper War of 1786-1788; a Bibliographical and Critical Inquiry Including an Account of the Origins of Protestant Ascendancy and its 'Baptism' in 1792*, Dublin, Irish Academic Press, 1993.

and the end of 1800. (What, one might ask by way of digression, is to be made of the emphasis in the Catholic archbishop of Dublin's observation in a letter of February 1799 about political assemblies of his co-religionists 'and their expectations of what is called emancipation'?[2]) But just as the issue debated then exceeded in immediate and long-term importance that which excited Richard Woodward and his contemporaries in 1786, so the list of pamphlets debating the union is ultimately of greater significance to historians. This is more than a matter of scale, it implicates a new formal dimension within debate. With the exception of the Glorious Revolution, no earlier event in Anglo-Irish relations had been so self-consciously historical than the union. The intervening decade-and-century had witnessed a revolution in intellectual activity, with history increasingly influential not so much as the hand-maid but as the fairy-godmother of politics. The local triumph of 1782 in Dublin merely served as a prelude to the greater drama at the end of the era. As in the greater *évenements* of 1789 and after, theatrical effect was sought at all costs. Yet the means to this end were more often dully prosaic.

2. 'THE SCOTTISH PLAY'

Prosaic, but by no means unplanned. While the structure of the present book distinguishes severely between research and reflection, presenting relatively bare bones in the list which follows, it should be emphasised that this division is a matter of presentation. It may seem that the details of pagination, implied dates and the rest of the data which can be gleaned from a physical examination of books and pamphlets, are the stuff of an uncomplicated empiricism. But reading emphatically is not an empirical activity in the sense that hearing or seeing is. And one must bear in mind that prior decisions about topic, theme and the interconnectedness of discrete instances of these have preceded the intellectual examination of each item, let alone its inclusion in the list. Or, to be more precise, decisions about theme etc are sustained throughout the business of compiling the list where the arrival of a new item can reveal previously unthought of implications in items long considered well-known and uncomplicated.

Consider a case in point. *Report on the Events and Circumstances which Produced the Union of the Kingdoms of England and Scotland* [2 vols London, 1799] was prepared for the duke of Portland. Similar compilations had been assembled in the past, to assist the authorities in the advancement of lesser schemes than a union of two kingdoms: a noteworthy feature of that under discussion was its printed state combined with its restricted circulation. The absence of a title-page suggests a wholly non-public circuit of distribution, and yet the requirement of print indicates the extensiveness of that orbit, which manuscript transmission could not economically serve.

[2] J. T. Troy to Sir J. C. Hippisly, 9/2/1799, quoted in Charles Vane (ed.) *The Memoirs and Correspondence of Castlereagh* ... (London, 1848) vol 2 p. 172.

A manuscript note on the printed copy presented by John Bruce to Portland reads in part as follows:

> When the question of Union between Great Britain and Ireland came under the consideration of His Majesty's Ministers the Duke of Portland employed Mr Bruce, the Keeper of the State Papers, to collect in his Office the Precedents in the History of the Union between England and Scotland which might illustrate the Subject, for the purpose of bringing, in aid of the intended arrangement with Ireland, the Wisdom and experience of former times, by which investigations it will appear that many of the Arguments which were brought against the Union with Scotland, and which time has completely refuted, are the same with those on which the Opponents of an Union with Ireland at present rely.[3]

It is therefore not surprising that the anonymous *Arguments for and against an Union*, Dublin Castle's spearhead contribution to the paper war, is pithy on the question of Scottish precedents. Indeed, these precedents constitute something of an unnamed presence in a quite a number of the pamphlets listed, unnamed in the same jocular-superstitious way that actors avoid uttering the play-title *Macbeth*, and by a complimentary gesture wish each other well with the phrase, 'break a leg.' Reprints of Daniel Defoe's writings on the Union of 1707 rubbed shoulders with intensely local and contemporary argument. But if one had not looked at Bruce's printed compendium, had not overcome a tendency to regard it as an internal document despite its printed form, then Defoe would have seemed wholly external to the union debates.

3. THE PROLOGUE

The *Arguments*, just referred to, remains the most baffling item in the list. Immediately identified as the deliberate initiative of Dublin Castle in the business of promoting an union, it was also recognised as the work of Edward Cooke (1755–1820).[4] Given the high level of its authorisation, one is somewhat puzzled to find that it was published in two quite distinct forms, both appearing above the name of John Milliken, a prominent Dublin bookseller with an address in Grafton Street. These may be distinguished as the 'December 1798' imprint and the '1799' imprint respectively. (There were, of course, London issues deriving from these, and Cork ones also, not to mention a spectral Dublin piracy.) We learn from a variety of sources that Cooke's anonymous pamphlet was first published on Monday 3 December 1798. But why should a bookseller, or even so powerful an authorial agency as the Castle, go to the trouble of dating one (but only one) set

---

[3] Dated Whitehall 15th Feb 1799, this formal memorandum is bound at the front of BL: 601 e 12. I am grateful to Brian Jackson for his discussion of the matter.
[4] For a succinct biographical note on Cooke, see Vane (ed.) op. cit. vol 1 pp. 314-315.

of 'editions' to the month of December, when convention very rarely allowed for any more specific dating than that of the year in question? And why should there be a second set of 'editions', dated 1799, and appearing from the same bookseller? These questions deserve attention, not just as technical details of the print business, but as aspects of a major ideological drive to shape a public opinion in Ireland.

It is well known that booksellers, issuing a publication in December, often dated it to the following calendar year. Thus, in the celebrated instance already discussed, Richard Woodward's *Present State of the Church of Ireland*, in practice issued on 18 December 1786, bore the date 1787.[5] The reason for this temporary inaccuracy probably related to a reluctance to see a book 'age' within a few weeks so that it seemed to be a product of the previous year when it was in fact but a few weeks, or even a few days, off the press.[6] In this way, it could be said that Cooke's pro-union pamphlet got the best of both worlds; it was linked firmly and immediately to the year of the Rebellion (which concentrated minds on the extremity of the situation in Ireland) while also sustaining itself into a year of sales, replies, and further editions. But why two distinctly dated versions? Who conceived this strategy – the author or the bookseller, Dublin Castle or market forces? Was the scale of the pamphlet debate on the issue of a possible union between Ireland and Great Britain desired, predicted, even planned, at the time of Cooke's publication? Are these questions, based as they are on a notion of human agency, irrelevant to the historian?

4. NUMBERS

In 1799, before the matter was decided, Milliken (an energetic figure in the market-place, a manufacturer of books with whom no author could compare in productivity) issued a list of union pamphlets published by himself: of the forty-nine items concerned, seventeen were in favour of a union, and thirty-two against. There are other estimates; the editor of Viscount Castlereagh's *Correspondence* (1848) observed that, following Cooke's *Arguments*, 'not fewer than thirty pamphlets on the subject were published in Ireland before the end of the year.'[7] When G. C. Boulton considered the matter in *The Passing of the Irish Act of Union* (1966), he accepted an estimate of 'some fifty' as the number of all pamphlets debating the issue and published by whatever bookseller; of these fifty, 'no more than ten are written in favour of Union'. That total figure, implausible even then, is here multiplied by a factor of 6+.[8] It is true that Boulton was more

[5] See *The Dublin Paper War*, pp. 50-62.
[6] The practice lasted well into the Victorian age and, in the case of 'annuals' for children, persists even in the mid- to late- twentieth century.
[7] Vane (ed.) vol 1 p. 154.
[8] G. C. Boulton, *The Passing of the Irish Act of Union; a Study in Parliamentary Politics*, Oxford, Clarendon Press, 1966, p. 77 n3. His source is R. B. MacDowell, *Irish Public Opinion 1750-1880*, London, Faber, 1944. In fairness to Boulton, his tally may be based on a shorter 'run-up' to the union decision than that taken as the base of the present listing.

concerned with what was going on inside parliament than with the activities of anonymous pamphleteers and their booksellers. And since the 1940s when R. B. MacDowell's *Irish Public Opinion* began to open up new areas of inquiry, and the 1950s when most of Boulton's research was carried out, much has changed in the methods and concerns of historians. The concept of public opinion has been given greater rigour, though not conspicuously in Irish discussions of it.[9] And if pamphlets are thought of more highly now, so too the decade in which union became the dominant issue of political debate has become the focus of hyperactive attention among centenary-conscious researchers. Few of them will complain if latter-day political controversies give their learned publications an additional appeal.

Pro and Con – the title of a summary pamphlet issued by Marchbank in 1800 – might be thought to summarise also the starkly few classifications under which this vast body of material might be analysed. But this would involve a capitulation to manifest content as found in many – but not, in fact, all – of the publications themselves, without consideration of other (latent, if you like) possibilities. These are unlikely to emerge in any comprehensive fashion from the present list, the interim status of which will be discussed in a moment. But already, additional schema of analysis can be discerned – some examples are the distinctions between

 i) anonymous and signed pamphlets;
 ii) printed parliamentary speeches and publications originating wholly outside the Irish Lords and Commons;
 iii) pamphlets exclusively published in Ireland and those issued (or re-issued) in Great Britain;
 iv) Dublin publications and those issued elsewhere in Ireland;
 v) material originally published before – even long before – the critical years of 1797-1800 though re-issued in that later context, and that which is composed within the period indicated in the title of the present work;
 vi publications clearly issued in more than one state (whether revised or not) and those which apparently had a unique issue;
 vii) the solemn and the satirical;
 viii) prose and verse ...

For the present, however, any extended comparison remains implicit as the business of establishing precisely what was published awaits completion.

The preliminary alphabetical title-list attempts to bring together in a single sequence all the separate publications, appearing between January 1797 and the end of 1800, which discussed a possible union between the kingdoms of Ireland and Great Britain. Similar proposals had been voiced in the past, but the debate in the late 1790s differed from earlier occasions, not least because union was effected on 1 January 1801. Even taking into account the historian's legitimate

---

[9] The most notable critique is Jurgen Habermas' *Structural Transformation of the Public Sphere* (1962) which unfortunately remained untranslated into English until 1989.

acknowledgement that the outcome of an extended event alters one's apprehension of its early development, we should still emphasise that the 1790s discussion of union differed massively in scale from any previous exchange of pamphlets.[10] Nor was this contrast directly the consequence of the issue at stake's being greater; on the contrary, the capacity of the printing presses, and of Dublin's book trade generally, to generate a far greater volume of pamphlet material contributed to the enlargement of the debate. This material difference in the size of the medium of communication undoubtedly affected the message.

5. ANONYMITY AND PSEUDONYMITY

Even if it is allowed that the present list is preliminary, and that its users will extend and refine it, some interim judgements may be attempted. I am aware that the issue was discussed in *fora* distinct from the pamphleteering market – in parliament itself, newspapers, county meetings, polite literature, political societies (a relatively new phenomenon), religious bodies and so forth. I am also conscious that union did not occur solely (or even principally) as the consequence of discussion. It was effected and resisted structurally as well as discretely; it was both determined and managed; indeed the manner of its final passage through the parliaments admirably illustrates the old chestnut of freedom and necessity, which Lucien Goldmann's concept of transindividual agency can help to illuminate. The present concentration on pamphlets is thus a limited one, which nonetheless directs attention to a point of intersection where all sorts and conditions of men (with at least one woman) met together on whatever terms of inequality as participants in the struggle for public opinion.

The code of anonymity, though it was by no means universal and certainly held no charms for MPs keen to air their views outside the House, ensured that the authors of these works did not in any general sense know each other. Of course, some pamphlets were signed – the present list would indicate a relatively high proportion. And undoubtedly, the authorship of others was an open secret: in this respect, Ireland differed very markedly from the *ancien régime* conditions described by Arlette Farge in her study of public opinion in pre-revolutionary France.[11] It is also pretty clear that pamphlets were sometimes issued without the active consent – even knowledge – of the author of the material published. Thus the notion of authorship itself provides an opportunity to test the range and

---

[10] For a classic study of a major eighteenth-century political revolution, conducted principally through an examination of the role of pamphleteering, see Bernard Bailyn, *The Ideological Origins of the American Revolution*, Cambridge, Mass., Belknap Press, 1967.
[11] Arlette Farge, *Subversive Words; Public Opinion in Eighteenth-Century France*, Cambridge, Polity Press, 1994. First published in French in 1992, this study of clandestine journalism, police surveillance, rumour, and political voyeurism lies closer in its material to the mother of all Irish paper wars, that involving Jonathan Swift's *Drapier Letters* in 1724/5 than to events in the 1780s and '80s. See Patrick Kelly, 'Jonathan Swift and the Irish Economy in the 1720s', *Eighteenth-Century Ireland / Iris an dá Chultúr*, 6, (1991), pp. 7-36.

configuration of public opinion in late eighteenth-century Ireland.

Among the titles listed below, one which suggests itself in this connection is *A Reply to the Memoire of Theobald Mc Kenna ...* (1799). On the title-page authorship is indicated by the words, By Molyneux. The British Library cataloguer assigns the item to Sir Capel Molyneux; R. D. C. Black, in a reference work to which all researchers continue to be indebted, prefers William Philip Molyneux, later 1st baron Sefton. Both of these authorities have opted, in effect, to interpret the author-statement as transparent, though incomplete in lacking a fore-name, and they diligently seek to identify the particular member of the Molyneux family whom they believe most likely to have written the pamphlet. But an annotation on the fly-leaf of a bound volume of union pamphlets in Trinity College, Dublin, attributes it to 'Thomas Grady, chairman of Limerick County', and in doing so the unknown cataloguer has interpreted the printed author-statement as a pseudonym, deriving from the celebrated William Molyneux (1656-1698), whose *Case of Ireland's being Bound by Acts of Parliament in England Stated* had been burned by the common hangman one hundred years earlier than the pamphlet under discussion. Pseudonymity, in this instance, was a powerful component of the political argument, serving to remind historically-attuned readers of a century-long 'tradition' of what has been termed colonial nationalism, commencing with Molyneux, including Swift and Berkeley, and entering into its climactic crisis in the union debates. The 'tradition' of course is at once invoked and augmented by such a device, compared to which no single author could hold up his candle without blushing.

Prohibitions, whether strictly legal or imposingly conventional, did have their impact. The reporting of parliament's business was a case in point, perhaps the most important. The *Parliamentary Register* annually provided a detailed account of the proceedings of – mainly – the House of Commons, but its manner of presentation was not standard, utilising sometimes direct and sometimes indirect speech, together with occasional instances of the tersest summary. Reports of quasi-public occasions naturally varied in what we might term 'quality' – though it should be remembered that the notion of comprehensive reproduction of the *ipsissima verba* lay some time in the future. A copy of the *Report of the Debate of the Irish Bar ... 9th December 1798*, preserved in the library of the Royal Irish Academy, carries a manuscript note on its half-title reading 'said to have been taken down with particular care & attention'. On the other hand, the publisher of *A Report of Two Speeches ... by ... Castlereagh* admitted in his Advertisement (p. [iii]) that it was 'but a very inadequate outline of what was actually delivered'. Quite who the publisher was in this instance, or what kind of activity deserves that description, is not easy to say: in the particular case of Castlereagh's two speeches, the pamphlet was 'printed by Graisberry & Campbell for J Milliken'. When the role of publisher finally emerged in the space – as the current jargon would have it – between printer and book-seller, a further extension of the public domain was accomplished.

6. SOME REMARKS ON THE ORGANISATION OF THE LIST

Public domain – this defines the context in which it is worth clarifying what purpose the compiler envisages the preliminary alphabetical title list as serving, for it cannot be assumed that all readers will use it in the same way. Fundamentally, the material assembled here serves to reveal the manner in which an issue of high politics came to pervade a middling level or stratum of the public domain. Though bibliographical methods of description have been employed they have not been pressed home to the kinds of end which the professional bibliographer would expect. No collations have been attempted, partly because the physical survival of the pamphlets in bound volumes frustrates the examination of gatherings, cancels etc, and partly because any such examination of all the material would take a greater deal of time than any reseacher can afford. Nevertheless, much attention have been given to the identification of different states of what the professional historian would regard as the same text: these states are sometimes distinguished here by a mere variant spelling on a title-page (honorable or honourable) or by a claim of 'second edition', or (in properly substantive cases) by a new setting of type and/or a new imprint.

1 Sources

As it stands the list must be read at several distinct levels. Its references to copies preserved in Trinity College Dublin and in the Royal Irish Academy are based on a first-hand inspection of the items listed, though no collations have yet been attempted. References to items in the British Library, Cambridge University Library and the National Library of Ireland relate to an extensive but by no means complete survey of the items themselves, usually involving first-hand inspection. In the case of the Bodley Library, work commenced when (late in 1994) the new computerised on-line catalogue was introduced: first-hand inspection continues. Much of the relevant material in the University Library, Cambridge, is also accessible through the three-volume catalogue of the Bradshaw Collection. Naturally, copies in other libraries have been inspected as the opportunity arose, notably in Belfast where the Linenhall Library and the Foster Collection in the library of Queen's University contain small but interesting bodies of material. The Russell Library, in Saint Patrick's College, Maynooth, proved particularly fruitful.

Undoubtedly, many further copies can be traced. *The Eighteenth-Century Short Title Catalogue* will indicate holdings at further libraries in the British Isles and North America, and so will direct readers of the present work to repositories close to their homes. Where it has not proven possible to cite an example of a rare work by giving a call number in one of the major libraries listed above, a holding in some other (usually American) repository is provided. But, given the intensely local nature of some of the material, it is likely that smaller libraries in Ireland will throw up examples which are not to be traced through the great libraries of the world. Provincial printings – in Belfast, Cork, Limerick etc. – are probably underrepresented in the list as it stands.

11 Inclusion and exclusion

The union was so extensively discussed that the business of identifying those
publications involved in the debate might be thought the least of the problems
facing researchers. But the question was neither isolated from the longer-standing
debates of eighteenth-century politics nor from the 'single-issue' pronouncements
of seven-day wonder-workers. Thus a pamphlet announcing itself as a disquisi-
tion on trade, on the status of nuns, on the character of Henry Grattan, or on
rights for Catholics can turn out to be in substance a contribution to the debate
on union. Members of parliament, speaking on motions formally devoted to
procedural matters, were often addressing the larger issue and seeing their speeches
later circulate in pamphlet form. There is, of course, an extensive account of the
parliamentary debates on union printed in the annual volumes of the *Parliamentary Register*, but these have been excluded from the list on the grounds that their
issue was serial, that is, was predicated upon a programme of publication
established well before 1797 and upon considerations distinguishable from those
of union *per se*. Parliamentary material – e.g. *Speech of the Right Honourable ...*,
Substance of the Speech ... etc. – is included when its dissemination is clearly
intended (by the member or by a bookseller) to be a distinctive, separate item
circulating in the public domain.

Some material, newly issued between 1797 and the end of 1800 but originating
earlier, is included when its relevance to the current debate appears undeniable –
for example, several works devoted to Scottish affairs at the time of the union
with England. A subjective element is undoubtedly at work in these decisions to
include – what about editions of Swift or Molyneux in circulation during the
same period, where intention cannot be vested in an author? As it happens, there
does not appear to have a re-issue of the latter's *Case of Ireland's being Bound by
Acts of Parliament in England Stated* (1698) in the period under examination here:
perhaps the edition of – significantly – 1782 (BLACK 1205) is the nearest in time.
It is advisable at times to notice what is not published.

It also instructive to note how early cataloguers, librarians, binders, and owners
have classified material. For example, a bound volume of pamphlets in the Cambridge University Library (Hib. 5. 798. 1) has the following as its two first items:

[1] The speech of the right honourable John, lord baron Fitzgibbon (now
    earl of Clare) lord high chancellor of Ireland, delivered in the house of peers
    on the second reading of the bill for the relief of his majesty's Roman
    Catholic subjects March 13th 1793; with An accurate account of the speech
    of the right honourable John Foster, speaker of the House of Commons on
    the above subject February 27th 1793. London: printed for J Wright, 1798.
    42pp.

[2] An accurate report of the speech of the right hon. John Foster speaker of
    the House of Commons on the Roman Catholic bill Feb 27 1793. Dublin:
    printed by R Marchbank for J Milliken, 1798. 24pp.

Not only is the volume labelled as containing pamphlets on the Irish union, a contemporary hand has summarised these two items in a fly-leaf list of contents as 'Clare and Foster on the union'. Thus, at least one assessor of these five-year-old republished speeches on Catholic relief deemed them as dealing with the union. On reflection, a decision to exclude the two republications of 1793 speeches seemed the better alternative. Nevertheless, in the case of Foster – in whom inconsistencies of attitude were eagerly detected by his opponents – there is evidence of material being printed and distributed during the union exchanges, if not against his will then certainly in a manner which he considered unsatisfactory and even (perhaps) mischevous. For this reason, together with the unexpected quantity of matter appearing under his name, the Speaker is given – along with Edward Cooke – more than the bare-bones treatment in the list following.

To balance the issue of resurrected earlier publications, the *terminus ad quem* (1800) has been ignored in one or two instances, to allow the inclusion of some material appearing in 1801 which is germaine to the debate about the union as a proposition rather than to any reflection (whether supportive or hostile) on the union as an accomplished fact. Again, the subjective element cannot be discounted, but the number of instances is very small and the compiler's intention has been simply to ensure that what might be useful is not excluded on a chop-logic basis.

One category of publication which has not been considered in its own right is the issue of union pamphlets as collective sets under the imprint of John Milliken. These sets of *Union Tracts* are familiar to any explorer in the broken up libraries of nineteenth-century Irish 'big houses', but the mechanisms lying behind their manufacture or at least distribution as intellectual furniture cannot be considered here and now. The implications requiring close examination – involving the availability of unsold pamphlets in some quantity, or the piracy of other booksellers' work – are better addressed after the present interim list of individual publications has been absorbed and amended in the light of subsequent research. These sets, however, do contribute to the theatrical, and self-consciously historical, aspects of the union debates generally, by providing impressively bound testimony to the importance of the occasion.

III *The order of the list*

Pamphlets are listed on a word-by-word (as distinct from a letter-by-letter) alphabetical basis. Thus *Sketch of* ... precedes *Sketches*... Both the indefinite and definite articles are ignored, whether appearing as the first word in a title or in some subsequent position. There are a few occasions when it is uncertain what exactly the title of a particular publication may be: one such relates to brief items like songs, ballads etc where nothing as formal as a title-page occurs, and the opening words of the text itself have been highlighted in some typographical manner so as to serve in its stead; another involves the presence of the term 'union' itself, appearing at the top of a title-page more as a heading than as an integral part of the title of the individual work. Instances of the latter kind are indicated by {Union} or {The union} etc, with the item's alphabetical place determined by the word following the curly bracket.

At the risk of overstating something less than obvious, it should be noted that the list is organised round titles rather than texts. Thus, the distinction is maintained where the same text (substantially) is issued under variant titles (e. g. *Cease your Funning* and *Cease your Funning. The Rebel Detected* and {*The Union.*} *Cease your Funning* ... Apart from the need to establish some consistency of treatment across a body of highly diverse material, this decision is part and parcel of the underlying intention of the project as a whole, which is to demonstrate the *extent* to which print technology was mobilised in these years to saturate the literate public domain. A multiplicity of titles – linked to an unchanging, or little altered, text – contributed to that effect of saturation.

iv Bibliographical description

Purists may lament my failure to adopt the standards prescribed by Fredson Bowers and others in the matter of transcribing title-pages. To have done so would have required the signalling of line-endings in the title, the use of variant type-faces (italic, hollow letters etc.), the presence of mottoes, roman rule and other printers' devices. Such detail is usually only provided in accounts of the work of an individual author or printer where an *a priori* principle has been adopted of describing an ideal copy of each work in question. But, though a degree of bibliographical acumen has been maintained throughout, the overall objective has been to establish the external effect rather than the internal (print-room) means.

Consequently, the procedures adopted must be described with some precision.

1. Titles as rendered in the list are given always in roman type, and are transcribed verbatim, but punctuation is minimised in the service of conveying their fluent meaning, rather than their visual arrangement. (Nonetheless, punctuation variants, changing hyphens etc., may be recorded by a [sic] and/or in a note below the description proper to indicate the existence of multiple states of a title.) Lower case initials are used except
   i) for proper nouns (restrictively defined) and
   ii) to indicate the first word of a publication title incorporated within the title under description.
In the transcript the title concludes with a period.

2. The author statement (if any is present on the title-page) follows, in the form 'By ...' irrespective of the whether the preposition (or its like) is present and omitting (except in rare, important cases) additional palaver about the author.

3. The imprint follows in three stages –
   i) place of publication followed by a colon
   ii) then the name and role (printed for, sold by etc.) of the book-seller, printer or publisher as given (but without a period after initials, ie. J Milliken rather than J. Milliken and without details of address) and concluding with a comma

iii) then the date in arabic numerals in all cases no matter whether roman had
been used, and with inferred dates given in square brackets and this
concluding with a period.

These procedures for the imprint are designed to facilitate the following style of
machine reading – the word immediate preceding a colon is the place of
publication: the word immediately preceding the comma names the agent of
publication, and the term immediately preceding the full stop or period is the
date in years standardised to arabic. Inevitably, there are occasions (as with
London reprints) where the procedure has had to be modified.

v. The pragmatics of pagination

The vexed matter of pagination follows the imprint, and it requires somewhat
extended discussion. Ideally, a bibliographical account should provide a specific
figure for the total number of pages which passed through the printing press
irrespective of whether the concluding pages of the last gathering bear print or
not. This would also distinguish between preliminary pagination (often in small
roman numbers) and the pagination of the text proper (generally given in arabic
numbers.) Here, however, pagination is thought of as a characteristic summarised
in the final page-number, by which the conclusion of the text or publication can
be established.

For eighteenth-century books it would also be proper to provide a collation
expressed through the format (octavo or whatever) of the book and its constituent
gatherings as indicated (or otherwise) by signature letters. With very few
exceptions pamphlets of the status described here – flimsy in their original
condition, brief in extent (generally) and mutilated (to some extent or other) in
their present condition – have rarely earned this degree of very time-consuming
attention. Indeed, the practice of bringing a dozen or more pamphlets into a
single, tightly-bound volume has greatly frustrated the collation of this material.
As there is no *Areopagitica* to be found among the works under analysis – not
even *A Modest Proposal* – and as world enough and time are not on tap, I have
adopted a procedure which, following the American philosopher C. S. Peirce
(1839-1914), I want to call pragmaticist. Some explanation is necessary.

In reaction to the practice of William James and others, who took Peirce's
concept of pragmatism to involve a theory of truth, Peirce in 1905 coined the ugly
term pragmaticist to denote his own original project, which was to – 'Consider
what effects, which might conceivably have practical bearings, we conceive the
object of our conception to have. Then our conception of these effects is the
whole of our conception of the object.' Now our object here is the ideal copy,
which is to say it is a synthetic object tangible only in the description obtained
through inspection of as many examples as possible. But these examples are
identified on a working presumption that they *are* examples of the specific
edition/state in question, and so a circular (no prejorative implication in this)
procedure evolves.

In practice, it is has been deemed adequate to scrutinise the – usually quite numerous – copies of a given pamphlet preserved in the libraries of Trinity College and the Royal Irish Academy before coming to a provisional statement of its pagination. Naturally, revision of the resulting number is borne in mind as other copies elsewhere are examined. But as many – almost certainly a majority – of the examples generally available have suffered some damage or other, and as that damage most frequently afflicts the final leaves, one's findings remain provisional. To take a hypothetical example, it is wholly possible that all examinable examples of a given pamphlet survive in a condition which lacks the final leaves bearing advertisements, because librarians or book-binders over the years have not (until recently and in limited instances) taken such apparently extra-textual matter seriously. Thus, a unanimous conclusion as to the pagination of this example may yet be inaccurate in relation to some ideal copy. It is inevitable that, in the list which follows, the initial bibliographical description of a pamphlet may conclude with a statement of pagination which is at odds with a detail recorded below beside the call-mark for an individual example. Doubtless, the response of readers to the present work can help to eliminate some of these discrepancies, but the ideal copy remains something of an enigma, the end-point of a circular process. Declared paginations, therefore, are pragmaticist. And yet the underlying supposition of the present work as a whole is that historical truth can be sought, through a rigorous critique of empirical and pragmaticist findings.

vi Annotations and call numbers
The following codes are used:
BL = British Library, London
Bod = Bodley Library, Oxford
CUL = Cambridge University Library
DJ = Dublin Journal
DCPL = Dublin Corporation Public Library (Pearse Street)
NLI = National Library of Ireland, Dublin
RIA = Royal Irish Academy, Dublin (HP = Halliday Pamphlets : HT = Halliday Tracts.)
RLM = Russell Library, Saint Patrick's College, Maynooth
TCD = Trinity College, Dublin
UCC = University College, Cork
(A small number of libraries (American for the most part) are named in full, principally because each name rarely appears more than once.)

Where possible, and bearing in mind the interim status of the present work, I have endeavoured to record evidence of authorship without conceding that such a notion should have paramountcy. Though it is no negligible matter to encounter evidence that the enigmatic John Fitzgibbon wrote a pamphlet stated to be 'By Paddy Whack ...', a concern for the structure of public opinion and the public sphere should not allow the detective motive to predominate. A scanning of advertisements in the *Dublin Journal* has provided evidence tending to date a substantial proportion of items, but much remains to be done in this area. In other regards, annotation has been held in check, though internal evidence which might help to pin-point a time of publication has been recorded.

It is a feature of the pages below that call marks for major libraries are given for immediate access by librarians, bibliographers and others willing to confirm, correct, or expand the present work, and by those for whom it will (I hope) be a useful tool for their own research into an important period of Irish and British history. In addition, the following citation is provided where applicable – BLACK (followed by a serial number) indicates an entry in R. D. Collison Black, *A Catalogue of Pamphlets on Economic Subjects 1750-1900 and now housed in Irish Libraries*, Belfast, Queen's University, 1969.

Many people have assisted me in the research resulting in the present publication. I want to thank Robin Alston of the British Library (London) together with the staff of the Department of Older Printed Books (Trinity College, Dublin), the King's Inns Library (Dublin), the librarian of the Gilbert Collection (Dublin Corporation Public Libraries), the library of University College Cork, the Linenhall Library (Belfast), National Library of Ireland, the Rare Books Department (Cambridge University Library), the Royal Irish Academy, the Russell Library (Saint Patrick's College, Maynooth), and the Upper Reading Room (Bodley Library, Oxford). Stop-press thanks are richly due to Margaret O'Donnell of the Computer Help-Desk, Goldsmiths College. A research grant provided by the College allowed me to travel widely in the United Kingdom inspecting copies of neglected pamphlets. Finally, I want to thank Michael Adams of Irish Academic Press for his sustained interest in and commitment to my work.

Readers are cordially invited to send their annotations, complaints, and suggestions to the name and address subscribed, in anticipation of an expanded edition.

W. J. Mc Cormack,
Department of English,
Goldsmiths College,
Lewisham Way,
New Cross,
London, SE14 6NW

AN ANNOTATED ALPHABETICAL TITLE-LIST
OF THE PAMPHLETS WITH CALL NUMBERS
FOR COPIES PRESERVED IN THE MAJOR
LIBRARIES OF THE BRITISH ISLES

A1 An abridgment of the speech of lord Minto in the House of Peers, April 11 1799, on a motion for an address to his majesty, to communicate the resolutions of the two houses of parliament respecting an union between Great Britain and Ireland. Dublin: printed for J Milliken, 1799. 48pp.

RIA: HT 318/6 • BL: 1509/878

A2 An account of the proceedings of the merchants, manufacturers and others concerned in the wool and woolen trade of Great Britain in their application to parliament that the laws respecting the exportation of wool might not be altered in arranging the union with Ireland but left to the wisdom of the imperial parliament if such a measure should hereafter appear to be just and expedient. London: printed by W Phillips, 1800. 318pp.

BLACK 2188   RIA: HT 334/14 • BL: 958 k 25 • Bod: G Pamphlets 1463

A3 An accurate report of the speech of William Saurin esq. in the Irish House of Commons on Friday the 21st of February 1800 on the question of a legislative union with Great Britain. Dublin: printed by J Moore, 1800. 24pp.

BLACK 2272   TCD: Crofton 209/5 • RIA: HT 335/25 • RIA: HT 335/8
BL: 287 g 14 (8) • Bod: G Pamphlets 1947/5

A4 An act for the union of Great Britain and Ireland, Friday the first day of August, one thousand eight hundred, royal assent given. John Gayer, D. Cler. Part. Dublin: printed by George Grierson, 1800. 118pp. + 8 sheets.

Note: issued in two states - i) with linen backing on the folded sheets (BL copy) and with paper sheets (DCPL copy).

DCPL: Gilbert 19 A 6/5 • BL: C. S. A. 21/13

A5 Address and resolutions of the two houses of parliament in Ireland, and accounts of the commerce and revenue of Great Britain and Ireland. Dublin: printed by George Grierson, 1800. xx, 100pp.

KID: N. 1. 22 (2)

A6 An address on the subject of the projected union to the illustrious Stephen III, king of Dalkey, emperor of the Mugglins, elector and archtreasurer of Lambay, lord protector of the holy island of Magee, grand duke of Bullock, grand master of the noble, illustrious, and ancient orders of the lobster, crab, scollop etc etc. By Patt. Pindar. Dublin: printed for the author and sold at 60 Stephen-street, 1799. 20pp.

Authorship: attributed to Henrietta Battier (1751?-1813) in the cataloque of the Crofton collection, TCD. likewise in the Gilbert Collection catalogue, DCPL.

TCD: Crofton 160/10 • RIA: HT 331/10 (very fragile)
NLI: P 4 • DCPL: Gilbert 19 E 6
House of Lords Record Office P.T. vol 4 no 2 (Peel Tracts)

A7 An address to the merchants, manufacturers and landed proprietors of Ireland in which the influence of an union on their respective pursuits is examined and in which the real reciprocal interests of Great Britain and Ireland are candidly and impartially discussed. By Nicholas Philpot Leader. Dublin: printed for James Moore, 1800. 98pp

Note: p. 97 wrongly numbered p73 in many (all?) copies of the first edition.

BLACK 2240   RIA: HT 339/9 • NLI: P 112/1 • NLI: P 612/12
BL: 1560/1256 (4) • BL: 1609/3763

third edition. By Nicholas Philpot Leader. Dublin: printed for James Moore, 1800. 98pp.

TCD: Lecky A 3 35 (5) • TCD: Crofton 208/4 • RIA: HT 335/28
BL: 8145 dd 54

A8 An address to the nations of Great Britain and Ireland on the projected union since rejected by the independent Irish parliament. By the earl of Stanhope. Dublin: printed by T Henshall, 1799. 8pp.

Date: Date line Jan. 21 1799 (in both states).
Authorship: Charles Stanhope (1753-1816), 3rd earl Stanhope - title-page.

TCD: V h 24 no. 17 • NLI: P 2/6 • KID: 45/13

Dublin: printed for J Moore, 1799. 8pp.

RIA: HT 316/4 • BL: 8146 f 34 (6)

A9 An address to the people of Ireland against an union in which a pamphlet entitled Arguments for and against that measure is considered. By a friend to Ireland. Dublin: printed by J Stockdale, 1799. 48pp.

Note: Errata on p. 47.
Authorship: attributed to Robert Orr, by Black.

BLACK 2134   TCD: Crofton 202/6 • RIA: HP 766/ 17 • RIA: HT 316/6
RIA: HT 326/7 • NLI: JP 3353 • NLI: P 251/7
NLI: P 621/16 • CUL: Hib. 7. 799. 1

with considerable alterations and additions. The second edition. By a friend to Ireland. Dublin: printed by J Stockdale, 1799. 52pp.

TCD: V h 21 no. 11 • TCD: 91 p 38 no. 14 • TCD: Lecky A 4 32 no. 7
RIA: HT 311/17 • RIA: HT 330/1) • NLI: P 212/8 • NLI: 621/17

BL: 8145 cc 60 • Bod: G Pamphlets 243/5 • CUL: Hib. 5. 798. 68 (6)

A10 An address to the people of Ireland on the projected union. By John Collis. Dublin: printed for James Moore, 1799. 18pp.

Date: 'Kinsale, January 1 1799' (p. [3]).

BLACK 2066   TCD: Crofton 205/8 • RIA: HP 787/ 10
                                    RIA: HT 319/5 • BL: 8146 f 34 (16)

Cork: printed by A Edwards, 1799. 24pp.

NLI: P 609/4

A11 An address to the people of Ireland on the subject of the projected union. By Thomas Goold. Dublin: printed by James Moore, 1799. 110pp.

Date: 'on Monday next will be published' (DJ Thursday 10/1/99, p. 3 col 4).
Authorship: Thomas Goold (1766?-1846) - title-page.
Note: RIA: HT 326/2 is Sir Jonah Barrington's copy - unannotated.

BLACK 2094   TCD: V h 23 no. 12 • TCD: 91 p 38 no. 12
                                    RIA: HT 317/11 • RIA: HT 326/3
                                    BL: 8145 de 10 (3) • Bod: G Pamphlets 1966/6

second edition. Dublin: printed by James Moore, 1799. 110pp.

RIA: HP 789/14 • RIA: HT 317/1 • RLM: PA 867/8

third edition. Dublin: printed by James Moore, 1799. 110pp.

RIA: HT 326/1 (final leaf damaged) • NLI: 611/7

fourth edition. Dublin: printed by James Moore, 1799. 110pp.

TCD: Lecky A 4 34 no. 17 • RIA: HT 320/7 • NLI: I 6551 Dublin (1799) 2

fifth edition. Dublin: printed by James Moore, 1799. 110pp.

TCD: Crofton 184/15 • TCD: Crofton 204/18
RIA: HT 326/2 • BL: 8146 f 34 (1)

A12 An address to the people of Ireland shewing them why they ought to submit to an union. Dublin: printed and sold by the book-sellers, 1799. 16pp.

Authorship: NLI attributes this item to Mary Emma (or Maryanne) Holmes (née Emmet), on the authority of R R Madden. BL & Bod attribute it to Roger O'Connor.

RIA: HP 787/ 15 • NLI: P 107/12 • BL: 8146 bbb 23 (1)
Bod: G Pamphlets 243/10 • Bod: 8 R 54/8 Th BS

A13 An address to the Roman Catholics of Ireland on the conduct they should pursue at the present crisis, on the subject of an union. By an old friend. Dublin: printed for J Moore, 1799. 8pp.

Date: date-line (p. 8) December 20th 1798.

TCD: V h 22 no. 7 • TCD: Lecky A 4 33 no. 9
TCD: 91 p. 13 (14) • RIA: HP 767/ 12 • RIA: HP 780/10
NLI: P 221/14 • NLI: P 2/10 • NLI: P 623/6
BL: 8145 de 8 (7) • BL: 8146 f 34 (15)

A14 Animadversions on the speeches of Mr Saurin and Mr Bushe etc etc. By William Smith. Dublin: printed and sold by Marchbank, 1800. 46pp.

Authorship: [Sir] William Cusack Smith (1766-1836, 2nd baronet) - title-page.

BLACK 2279   RIA: 805/8 • NLI: P 93/10 • NLI: P 153/6 • NLI: P 156/6
NLI: JP 351 • NLI: P 226/7 • BL: 1509/877

A15 The answer of Denis Feagan, breeches-maker at Edenderry, to the letter of Darby Tracy, chairman in St James's-street London, wherein is clearly proved the bad effects and misfortunes an union with Great Britain will have on the interest and happiness of the common people of Ireland. [By] Nabouclish. Dublin: printed for James Moore, 1799. 12pp.

Date: Signs off, p.12, Denis Feagan, Edenderry, Dec 23 1799.
Authorship: Preface signed (p. [3]) W. E.

BLACK 2081   TCD: Crofton 208/2 • RIA: HT 315/11 • NLI: JP. 425
NLI: I 6551 Dublin (1799) • BL: 8146 ff 50 • Bod: Vet A5 e 3418/2

A16 An answer to the pamphet entitled Arguments for and against an union etc etc, in a letter addressed to Edward Cooke esq., secretary at war. By Pemberton Rudd. Dublin: printed for J Milliken, 1799 [recte 1798]. 36pp.

Date: 'This Day is published' (DJ 18/12/98). A title-page ms. note on RIA HP: 766/5 reads '1st edn. 10 Decr 1798'.
Authorship: Pemberton Rudd (title-page).

BLACK 2152   TCD: V h 21 no. 5 • TCD: Crofton 182/5
TCD: Crofton 202/5 • TCD: Lecky A 4 32 no. 5
RIA: HP 766/5 • RIA: HT 317/13 • RIA: HT - Box 318/1
RIA: HT 326/4 • NLI: P 107/7 • NLI: P 212/9
NLI: JP 3340 • Bod: 226 i 168/13 • CUL: Hib. 7. 799. 40

third edition corrected. Dublin: printed for J Milliken, 1799. 36pp.

Date: 'also may be had the Third Edition of the first letter' (DJ 24/12/98 p.1 col. 4).

RIA: HT 326/6 • NLI: P 2/3 • NLI: P 251/4
Bod: G Pamphlets 2758/9 • Bod: G Pamphlets 2028/6

Cork: printed by J Connor, J Haly, and M Harris, 1798. 20pp.

Bod: G Pamphlets 1204/9

a new edition. London: re-printed for John Stockdale, 1798. 24pp.
(reads 'intituled') BL: 1103 k 6

A17 An answer to the pamphet entitled Arguments for and against an union etc etc, in letters addressed to Edward Cooke esq., secretary at war. Letter the second. By Pemberton Rudd. Dublin: printed for J Milliken, 1799. 34pp.

Date: Date-line, p. 33, 21 December 1798. 'at one o'clock this Day will be published' (DJ 22/12/98). A title-page ms. note on RIA: HP 766/6 reads '1st ed. 23d Decr 1798'.
Authorship: Pemberton Rudd - title-page.

BLACK 2153 TCD: V h 21 no. 6 • TCD: Crofton 182/6
TCD: Crofton 202/5 • TCD: Lecky A 4 32 no. 6
RIA: HP 766/6 • RIA: HT 317/12
RIA: HT 326/5 • BL: 1509/ 1178

A18 An answer to a pamphlet entitled The speech of the earl of Clare on the subject of a legislative union between Great Britain and Ireland. By Henry Grattan. London: printed for G G and J Robinson, 1800. 48pp.

Authorship: Henry Grattan (1746-1820) - title-page.

BLACK 2230 RIA: HP 806/9 • NLI: 611/8

Dublin: printed for J Moore, 1800. 44pp

TCD: Crofton 209/8 • TCD: Gall Z 1 95 (6) • RIA: HT 335/24
RIA: HT 336/13 • NLI: P 112/10 • BL: 8145 d 34

second edition. Dublin: printed for J Moore, 1800. 44pp.

RIA: HT 336/7 • NLI: P 611/9 • NLI: P 401/9

third edition. Dublin: printed for J Moore, 1800. 44pp.

RIA: HP 797/5 • RIA: HT 336/12 • NLI: P 226/3
NLI: P 611/10 • BL: 1103 g 8 (1) • Bod: 8 Y 84 Jur.

fourth edition. Dublin: printed for J Moore, 1800. 44pp.

RIA: HP 799/ 4 • RLM: PA 342/1

fifth edition. Dublin: prited for J Moore, 1800. 44pp.

NLI: JP 3352

fifth edition with considerable additions. Dublin: printed for J Moore, 1800. 52pp

RIA: HP 806/10 • RIA: HT 336/21 • RIA: HT 337/9 • NLI: P 611/11

Cork: printed by J Haly, 1800. 48pp.

RIA: HT 335/15 • Bod: G Pamphlets 1968/2

A19 An answer to some of the many arguments made use of against a pamphlet entitled Arguments for and against an union. By an attorney. Dublin: printed for J Milliken, 1799. 22pp.

Date: Date line, p. 22, January 1st 1799; advertised DJ 29/1/99 (p. 4 col. 4).
Authorship: attributed to 'James Galbraith esq Atty' in TCD: Crofton 184 fly-leaf list.

BLACK 2044   TCD: V h 24 no. 13 • TCD: Crofton 184/12
                          TCD: Crofton 204/13 • TCD: Lecky A 4 34 no. 13
                       RIA: HT 317/2 • RIA: HT 323/10 • RIA: HT 326/8
          NLI: Ir 94107 t 3 (3.13) • BL: 8146 f 34 (8) • BL: 1509/1173 (1)

A20 The anti-union. Dublin: printed by James Moore, 1798-1799. (32 issues, between 27/12/1798 and 9/3/1799 = 128pp.)

Note: TCD: V h 29 copy is bound with a list of voters in two colours, [4] pp. The Bod set lacks issues 10, 30, & 32.

TCD: Lecky A 7 38 (item 4) • TCD: V h 29
NLI: I 6551 Dublin 1798-9 • Bod: G Pamphlets 2201/1-19

A21 An appeal to the loyal citizens of Dublin. By a freeman of Dublin. Dublin: printed by John Milliken, 1800. 42pp.

Authorship: ms note on the flyleaf of TCD: Crofton 189 reads "An Appeal to the Citizens of Dublin was wrote by Ld. Bishop of Meath' [i.e. Thomas Lewis O'Beirne].

BLACK 2190   TCD: Crofton 189/12 • TCD: Crofton 209/10
                          RIA: HP 797/7 • RIA: HP 806/8 • NLI: P 621/15
                          CUL: Hib. 5. 800. 16 • CUL: Hib. 5. 800. 17

A22 An argument addressed to the yeomanry of Ireland demonstrating the right, the propriety, the utility and the obligation of declaring their sentiments on political subjects in their public distinctive character of yeomen. By Eunomus. Dublin: printed by J Stockdale, 1800. 32pp.

Note: see p. 20 re union.

TCD: Crofton 208/8 • RLM: PA 869/6 • BL: 8145 d 27

A23 An argument for independence in opposition to an union addressed to all his countrymen. By an Irish Catholic. Dublin: printed by J Stockdale, 1799. 52pp.

Authorship: W. J. Mac Neven. Attributed to 'Dr MacNevin' in TCD: Crofton 184 fly-leaf list.

BLACK 2122   TCD: V h 25 no. 2 • TCD: Crofton 184/13
                          TCD: Crofton 204/17 • TCD: Lecky A 4 34 no. 14
                  RIA: HT 323/8 • NLI: P 2/9 • BL: 1509/4606 • BL: 8145 e 2

Bod: G Pamphlets 243/6 • CUL: Hib. 5. 798. 68 (7)

A24 Arguments for and against an union between Great Britain and Ireland considered.

Date: 'At Two o'clock this Day will be published' (DJ Saturday 1/12/98 p. 2 col. 1). RIA: HP 766/1 bears ms note on the t-p 'first edition published Monday 3rd Decr 1798. CH'. An examination of some variants strongly suggests that Milliken's 1799 imprints preceded the December 1798 ones. Burnside's edition was a piracy.
A ms note on CUL: HIB 5. 799. 7 indicates 'Decr 6th 98' as a date of publication: this may refer to Wright's first issuing of a London edition or to publication of his 'sixth edition' (London). Unlike the Dublin editions, the chronology of Wright's London editions would appear to match the sequential order of imprint-dates - ie, first those bearing December 1798 and then those specified as 1799. As the body of the entry demonstrates, the publication of this item was a complex business.

Authorship: Edward Cooke (1755-1820), secretary for war Dublin Castle; see presentation copy RLM: PA 865/1.

a) Dublin imprints (i)
Dublin: printed for J Milliken, 1799. 58pp

TCD: OLS 186 n 25 (1) original state • TCD: OLS 186 n 25 (2) repaired
RIA: HT 316/9 • RIA: HT 317/16 • RIA: HT 332/8 • RIA: HT 333/6
NLI: JP 473 (untrimmed) • NLI: JP 4850 • NLI: P 616/5
NLI: P 156/1 • RLM: PA 865/1 (presentation copy)
RLM: PA 739/1 • BL: 111 d 49 • CUL: Hib. 5. 799. 5

second edition. Dublin: printed for J Milliken, 1799. 58pp.

Note: this was issued in at least two states, the later incorporating alterations on pp. 49, 50, 51 & 54. RIA: HT 332/9 is an example of the earlier and much rarer state.

TCD: Crofton 129/8 • RIA: HT 311/7 • RIA: HT 322/10
RIA: HT 332/9 • NLI: P 221/9 • NLI: P 616/6 • NLI: JP 3342
RLM: PA 42/5 • BL: 1103 g 10 (5) placed 6th in vol.
BL: 08139 ccc 48 (2) • Bod: G Pamphlets 2758/3
CUL: Hib. 5. 799. 2 • CUL: Hib. 5. 799. 3
CUL: Hib. 5. 799. 4 • CUL: Hib. 7. 799. 2

fourth edition corrected. Dublin: printed for J Milliken, 1799. 58pp.

Note: described in ESTC as ' a reissue of the second edition with a new title page', that is a reissue of the later state of the second edition.

RIA: HT 329/2 first item • NLI: P 107/6
BL: 8145 cc 21 • Bod: Vet A5 e 5659

fifth edition corrected. Dublin: printed for J Milliken, 1799. 58pp.

Note: all three inspected copies are poorly assembled.

RIA: HT 332/10 • KID: 42/1 • CUL: Hib. 5. 799. 6 (lacks pp. 51-55) sixth edition corrected. Dublin: printed for J Milliken, 1799. 58pp.

NLI: P 2/2 • NLI: P 616/7 • BL: 1509/1136

seventh edition corrected. Dublin: printed for J Milliken, 1799. 48pp.

RIA: HT 326/9 • NLI: P 251/1 • RLM: PA 876/3
BL: 1609/3677 • Bod: G Pamphlets 2758/4

b) Dublin imprints (ii)
sixth edition. Dublin: printed for T Burnside, 1798. 40pp.

Harvard University (Houghton Library): *EC75. c7745.798 af

c) Dublin imprints (iii)
eighth edition. Dublin: printed for J Milliken, December 1798. 62pp.

Note: ESTC notes that in some copies the t in 'against' is missing. The fly-leaf and t-p. of CUL: HIB 5. 798. 9 carry ms. note which concludes re this and other titles - 'very curious, scarce, & now not to be procured. I collected them with great difficulty & at considerable expence in 1803.' (unsigned).

TCD: V h 21 (1) • TCD: Crofton 182/1 (62pp. only)
TCD: Crofton 202/1 (62pp. + 1 blank leaf) • RIA: HP 766/1
NLI: P 360/11 (untrimmed) • NLI: P 401/4 (62pp text + blank final leaf)
NLI: P 616/9 (with half-title-page) • KID: 13/6 • Bod: G Pamphlets 243/1
CUL: Hib. 5. 798. 9 • BL: 8145 de 9 (1) (imperfect)

eighth edition. Dublin: printed for J Milliken, December 1798. 58pp.

RIA: HP 755/22 • RIA: HT 306/6 • BL: 8145 cc 20

ninth edition. Dublin: printed for J Milliken, December 1798. 62pp.

Note: The NLI copy has half-title of the eighth edition, title-page of the collective *Tracts on ... an Union vol 1* (Dublin: sold by J Milliken, 1799) and the title page of the ninth edition. That in TCD is similar though without a half-title-page.

TCD: Lecky A 4 32 (1) • NLI: Ir 94107 p 14 (4)

d) Cork Imprints
Cork: printed by M Harris, 1798. 28pp.

Free Lib. of Philadelphia: Cork 1798 Arguments 1.

second edition. Cork: printed by M Harris, 1798. 28pp.

NLI: I 6551 Cork 1798 (19 A)
Free Lib. of Philadelphia: Cork 1798 Arguments 2

e) London Imprints (see also A-25 below)
Arguments for and against an union between Great Britain and Ireland consid-

ered. [London:] Dublin printed: London re-printed for J Wright, December 1798. 60pp.

> BL: 1560/523 (2) • NLI: P 83/2 (58pp text) • RLM: PA 346/1
> CUL: Hib. 5. 798. 4 • CUL: Hib. 5. 798. 5 • CUL: Hib. 5. 798. 3/6

second edition. [London:] Dublin printed; London re-printed for J Wright, December 1798. 60pp.

Note: The Goldsmiths Collection copy is annotated in ms. throughout.

> RIA: HP 755/21 • DCPL: Gilbert 7 G 26 (5) • BL: 8145 b 36
> Bod: 22956 e 73/1 • CUL: Hib. 5. 798. 6
> CUL: Hib. 5. 798. 7 (lacks final leaf with ads.)
> Goldsmiths Collect.: 1798 (ser. no. 17, 223)

fourth edition. [London:] Dublin printed; London re-printed for J Wright, 1799. 60pp.

> BL: 117 h 15 (with half-title)

fifth edition. [London:] Dublin printed; London re-printed for J Wright, 1799. 60pp.

> BL: 111 d 50

sixth edition. [London:] Dublin printed; London reprinted for J Wright, 1799. 58pp.

Note: copy inspected has tipped-in leaf at back, with ms. quotes from reviews in *Critical Review* and *Anti-Jacobin Magazine*, similar to *Speech of Patrick Duigenan* - S20 below.

> CUL: Hib. 5. 799. 7

A25 Arguments for and against an union between Great Britain and Ireland considered to which is prefixed a proposal on the same subject by Josiah Tucker DD dean of Gloucester. London: re-printed for J Stockdale, 1798. 32pp.

Authorship: Edward Cooke (1755-1820) and Josiah Tucker (1712-1799) - title-page and evidence as for A24.

> NLI: P 119/2 • NLI: P 615/13 • BL: 8145 d 23
> Bod: G Pamphlets 1204/11

a new edition. London: re-printed for J Stockdale, 1798. 32pp.

> BL: T 1123 (5) • CUL: Hib. 5. 798. 8 • Bod: G Pamphlets 915/2

A26 At the royal circus near College-Green for the benefit of the great Mrs Britain on Monday February 3rd will be performed a grand serio-comic pastichio called The rape of Ierne, or fidelity betrayed etc. [Dublin, 1800] s sh fol

Note: copy inspected has ms key identifying notables such as Edward Cooke, Castlereagh,

Arthur Brown with disreputable roles in the performances.

CUL: Hib. o. 800. 3

A27 At the royal circus near College-Green for the benefit of the great Mrs Britain on Wednesday February 5 will be performed a grand serio-comic pastichio called The rape of Ierne, or fidelity betrayed etc. [Dublin, 1800] s sh fol

TCD: S ee 55 (4) • BL: 1325 g 15 (3) • CUL: Hib. o. 800. 1

A28 At the royal circus near College Green, for the benefit of Mrs Ireland on Wednesday January 15 will be performed a grand pantomimical serio-comic olio called The forced marriage; or the humbugged islanders. [Dublin, 1800] s sh fol.

TCD: S ee 55 (5) • BL: 1325 g 15 (1) • CUL: Hib. oo. 800. 1

B

B1 The blessings of union. [Song, 'How justly alarmed is each Dublin cit that he'll soon be transformed to a clown, Sir...'] Dublin: publish'd by Hime, [1800]. 4pp.

Note: in verse (7 stanzas).   BL: H 1653 j (65)

B2 A brief examination into the increase of the revenue, commerce and manufactures of Great Britain from 1792 to 1799. By George Rose. London: printed for J Wright [et al.], 1799. 78pp. + folding tables.

Authorship: George Rose (title-page).
Note: in addition to the states listed, CUL has printed material, being the introduction of this text, which is not from the same printing as the Dublin edition, nor is it from the so-called sixth or seventh London editions. See Hib. 7. 799. 14.

BLACK 2151, 2269   RLM: PA 597/3

from 1792 to 1799. Second edition. London: printed for J Wright [et al.], 1799. 78pp. + folding tables.

BL: 8247 b 39 • RIA: HT 332/1

from 1792 to 1799. Fifth edition. London: printed for J Wright [et al.], 1799. 78pp. + folding tables.

RLM: PA 577/4

From the corrected London edition, with an introduction by the Irish editor. By George Rose. Dublin: printed by Graisberry & Campbell, 1799. 78pp + folding tables.

TCD: Lecky A 4 36 (8) • RIA: HP 787/ 16 • RIA: HT 311/8

RIA: HT 311/8a • RIA: HT 321/17 • NLI: P 125/8

From the corrected London edition, with an introduction by the Irish editor. Third edition [half-title so describes it]. By George Rose. Dublin: printed & Graisberry and Campbell, 1799. xx, 77, [5] pp + folding tables.

TCD: Lecky A 4 36 (8) • TCD: 91 p 39 (1)

from 1792 to 1799. Seventh edition with considerable additions. By George Rose. Dublin: printed by John Exshaw, 1800. 82pp. + folding tables.

RIA: HP 803/1

C

C1 Calm considerations of the probable consequences of an union of the kingdom of Ireland with that of Great Britain. By Conciliator. Dublin: printed for J Milliken, 1799. 38pp.

Date: 'will be published in the ensuing week' (DJ 22/12/98 p. 3 col. 1 & 24/12/98 p. 1 col. 4)
Authorship: attributed to 'James Solas Dodd' in TCD: Crofton 184 fly-leaf list.

BLACK 2057   TCD: Crofton 184/6 (lacks t-p) • TCD: Lecky A 4 34 no. 6
RIA: HT 317/5 • RIA: HT 323/14

C2 The case of Ireland re-considered in answer to a pamphlet entitled "Arguments for and against an union considered". London: printed for the author, and sold by J Debrett, 1799. 86pp.

Authorship: attributed to Patrick Lattin, by Black. Ms note in TCD: Crofton 185 reads 'Mr Lattin of the County of Kildare'.

BLACK 2110, 2238   RLM: PA 1127/1 • Bod: G Pamphlets 915/3
CUL: Hib. 5. 799. 14 • CUL: Hib. 5. 799. 15
CUL: Hib. 5. 799. 16

[London:] printed by J Stockdale, 1800. 64pp.

TCD: Crofton 205/3 • RIA: HT 337/9 • NLI: 616/13

Dublin: printed from the author's edition published in London, by H Fitzpatrick, 1799. 64pp.

TCD: V h 25 no. 6 • RIA: HP 787/ 5 • NLI: 616/12 • BL: 8145 cc 59

London, printed; Dublin: re-printed by James Moore, 1799. 60pp.
Note: reconsidered without a hyphen.

TCD: 91 p 13 (12) • RIA: HT 322/15 • RIA: HT 325/2
RIA: HT 329/4 • NLI: 616/11 • BL: 8146 f 34 (3)

C3 Castle Rackrent; an Hibernian tale taken facts and from the manners of the Irish squires before the year 1782. [London:] printed for J Johnson by J Crowder, 1800. [4], xliv, 182pp.

Date: January, 1800.
Authorship: Maria Edgeworth (1768-1849), declared on post 1800 editions.

TCD: Lecky A 2 2 • BL: 12611 f 4 • CUL: S 727 d 80 25

second edition. London: printed by Luke Hansard for J Johnson, 1800. xvi, 214pp.

TCD: OLS 194 n 82 • BL: N 2494

Dublin: printed for P Wogan, H Colbert, P Byrne, W Porter, J Halpen, J Rice, H Fitzpatrick, G Folingsby, J Stockdale, R E Mercier and co., 1800. [2], xliv, 182pp.

TCD: OLS 194 o 77 • BL: 012635 b 83 • CUL: Hib. 7. 800. 98

C4 {Ireland}The Catholic question considered in a letter addressed to the editor of the Anti-Jacobin Review and Magazine. London: printed by Sampson Low, 1800. 52pp.

Note: a reply to L2 below. The title-page of Bod: G Pamphlets 1967/8 bears the ms inscription 'British Critic from the Author Messrs Rivingtons'.

RIA: HP 797/3 • RIA: HT 337/3 • BL: 111 e 4

C5 A caution to the inhabitants of Dublin. No. II. Dublin printed, 1799. 24pp.

TCD: Lecky A 4 36 (11) • BL: 8145 cc 14

C6 A caution to the inhabitants of Dublin. No. II. By an Irishman. Dublin: printed by John Exshaw, 1799. 16pp.

NLI: P. 1728/24 • NLI: I 6551 Dublin 1799

C7 A caution to the inhabitants of Dublin. No. III. By an Irishman. Dublin printed, 1799. 24pp.

Authorship: signed (p. 24) 'A Freeman of Dublin'.

NLI: JP 4856 • NLI: P 128/7

C8 A caution to the loyal inhabitants of Dublin. No. I. By a freeman of Dublin. Dublin printed, 1799. 20pp.

BLACK 2059   TCD: Lecky A 4 36 (10) • RIA: HT 315/12

C9 A caution to the loyal inhabitants of Dublin. No. II. By a freeman of Dublin. Dublin printed, 1799. 24pp.

Date: A ms. note, dated 14 February 1799, on the title-page of the NLI copy states that this was 'given about gratis and [is] literally the same as No. 3 by an Irishman published the 12th'.

NLI: P 621/14 • BL: 8145 cc 14

C10 A caution to the loyal inhabitants of Ireland. By an Irishman. Dublin: printed by J Exshaw, 1799. 14pp.   NLI: P 1728/23

C11 {The union.} Cease your funning. Dublin: printed by James Moore, 1798. 46pp.

Date: 'Bushe, Barrington and Mr Jebb come forth in print to-morrow.' Alexander Knox to Castlereagh, letter dated Friday [following 15/12/98], quoted in Castlereagh *Correspondence* (1848) vol 2 p. 45.

Authorship: Charles Kendal Bushe, see fly-leaf list in TCD:- Crofton 182. Black concurs.

BLACK 1998   RIA: HP 755/23 • NLI: JP 3355 • NLI: P 620/10

second edition. Dublin: printed by James Moore, 1798. 46pp.

NLI: P 620/11

C12 {The union.} Cease your funning; or, the rebel detected. Third edition. Dublin: printed by James Moore, 1798. 46pp.

Authorship: Charles Kendal Bushe (1767-1843) - see evidence for C11.
Note: with ads on p. 46.

TCD: V h 21 no. 14 • TCD: Crofton 129 (9) • RIA: HP 766/10
NLI: P 251/15 • RLM: PA 753/1 • BL: 1103 g 10 (4) (with half-title)
Bod: G Pamphlets 2758/1

fourth edition. Dublin: printed by James Moore, 1798. 46pp.

TCD: Crofton 129/9 • RIA: HP 766/ 11 • BL: 1509/523 (8)
Bod: G Pamphlets 1965 (5) • Bod: G Pamphlets 2758 (1)

fifth edition. Dublin: printed by James Moore, 1798. 46pp.

RIA: HT 303/2 • KID: 81/8

fifth edition. [Cork:] Dublin printed and Cork re-printed by Edwards, Harris and Connor, 1799. 24pp.

NLI: JP 293 • RLM: PA 35/12

seventh edition with a preface and notes by the author. Dublin: printed by James Moore, 1799. 48pp.

BLACK 2055   TCD: Crofton 182/10 • TCD: Crofton 202/9

TCD: Lecky A 4 32 no. 13 • RIA: HT 313/6 • RIA: HT 327/7
NLI: P 401/6 • NLI: I 6551 Dublin 1799 • Bod: G Pamphlets 243 (3)
CUL: Hib. 5. 799. 18

[London:] Dublin printed; London reprinted for J Debrett, 1799. 46pp.
DCPL: Gilbert 7 G 26 (4)
BL: 117 h 32 (with half-title) • BL : 111 e 1 (without half-title)
CUL: Hib. 5. 799. 17

C13 The commercial system of Ireland reviewed and the question of union discussed in an address to the merchants, manufacturers, and country gentlemen of Ireland. Dublin: printed by James Moore, 1799. 104pp.

Authorship: attributed to 'Rt Hon J: Foster' in TCD: Crofton 184 fly-leaf list. Accepted with a ? by Black.

BLACK 2086   TCD: V h 24 no. 9 • TCD: Crofton 204/16 • RIA: HT 320/6
NLI: P 5/3 • NLI: P 616/14 • BL: 1509/925

second edition with an introductory preface of. Dublin: printed by James Moore, 1799. 102pp.

Note: preface pp. iii-viii.

TCD: Crofton 184/14 • TCD: Lecky A 4 34 no. 16 • RIA: HP 789/13
RIA: HT 320/2 • RIA: HT 323/9 • NLI: 616/15 • BL: 8145 cc 61

C14 Competency of the parliaments of Great Britain & [sic] Ireland to incorporate their legislatures, with some remarks upon the debate in the Irish House of Commons upon the address. By the author of the "Necessity of an Incorporate Union between Great Britain and Ireland". Dublin: printed for J Milliken, 1799. 28pp.

Date: advertised DJ 5/3/99 p. 1 col 2.
Authorship: Milliken's advertisement for this and *Necessity* (DJ 5/3/99 p. 1 col. 2) concludes 'These last two pamphlets is [sic] generally attributed to the Pen of a Noble Lord formerly Secretary to L - d Car - le.' Ms note in TCD: Crofton 185 attributes this item to '—Nolan of Middle Temple'.
Note: RIA: HT 324/11 has list (p. 27) of pamphlets pub. by Milliken; TCD: Crofton 205/5 has similar list (pp. 27-28).

BLACK 2067   TCD: Crofton 205/5 • RIA: HP 787/ 7 • RIA: HT 324/11
BL: 8146 f 34 (2)

London: printed for J Wright, 1799. 44pp.

RLM: PA 1128/3 • BL: 117 h 34 • BL: 111 d 53 • CUL: Hib. 5. 798. 3/1

C15 Completion of the union etc. (drop title) 8pp.

TCD: Crofton 210/5 • RIA: HT 334/18

C16 The consequences of the proposed union with respect to Ireland considered, in a second letter to the marquis Cornwallis. By James Gerahty [sic]. London: printed for John Stockdale, 1799. 60pp. (+ 1 leaf of ads)

Authorship: James Geraghty - title-page where the surname is misspelled.

BLACK 2090   RIA: HT 316/10 • NLI: P 112/5 (no ads.)
                                              BL: 111 d 58 • BL: 117 h 35

C17 Considerations on the competency of the parliament of Ireland to accede to an union with Great Britain. By the right hon. Charles viscount Falkland. London: printed for J Wright, 1799. 22pp.

Authorship: Charles John Carey, viscount Falkland.

                                     BL: 117 h 33 • BL: 111 d 51

C18 Considerations on national independence suggested by Mr Pitt's speeches on the Irish union addressed to the people of Great Britain and Ireland. By a member of the Honourable Society of Lincoln's Inn. London: printed for Thomas Clio Rickman, [1799] 82pp.

Note: textually close to *Thoughts on national independence* - T5 below.

                          CUL: Hib. 5. 799. 24 • CUL: Acton C 54 13/4

C19 Considerations on the state of Ireland and the impolicy, impracticability of separation. Limerick: printed by Richard Peppard, 1799. 100pp.

BLACK 2069   RIA: HP 780/12

C20 Considerations upon the state of public affairs in the year MDCCXCIX. Ireland. Dublin: printed by W Porter and W Jones, 1799. 62pp.

Date-line, p. 62, London April 1799; 'This Day is Published' (DJ 30/4/99 p. 3 col 1). Authorship: attributed by BL to Thomas Richard Bentley, this accepted by Black: see also *Westminster School Register* (1892). Several NLI copies assigned to Richard Bentley, and TCD: Crofton 185 has 'Mr Bentley of London'. Below the publishing bookseller's advertisement in DJ, Milliken offers Auckland's *Substance* for sale, together with this item '(supposed) to be written by the above noble lord'. Milliken repeats this imputation in DJ 2/5/99 p. 2 col 1.

BLACK 2051   TCD: Lecky A 4 36 (9) • RIA: HP 786/4 • RIA: HT 319/6
                  RIA: HT 321/16 (with bookseller's adhesive label below imprint)
                  RIA: HT 324/10 • NLI: 617/2 • NLI: Ir 94107 p 14 (2)
                  UCC: Stopford Pamphlets 278 • BL: 8146 ee 23 (6)

Dublin: printed for J Milliken, 1799. 100pp.

                  TCD: Crofton 205/12 • RIA: HT 320/1 • NLI: P 5/4
                          NLI: 617/3 • BL: 1103 g 7 (3)

London: printed for F and C Rivington and J Hatchard, 1799. 100pp.

NLI: P 119/5 • CUL: Hib. 5. 798. 2/3

C21 The conspiracy of Pitt and co. detected in a letter to the parliament. By one of the people. Dublin: printed and sold by the book-sellers, 1799. 24pp.

TCD: V h 25 no. 8 • RIA: HT 319/4
RLM: PA 739/4 • BL: 8146 ee 23 (7)

C22 Constitutional considerations interspersed with political observations on the present state of Ireland. By Matthew Weld. Dublin: printed by J Moore, 1800. 80pp.

TCD: Lecky A 3 35 (4) • TCD: Crofton 208/3
RIA: HT 339/6 (authorial ms. note on t-p)

C23 Constitutional objections to the government of Ireland by a separate legislature in a letter to John Hamilton esq. occasioned by his remarks on a Memoire on the projected union. By Theobald M'Kenna. Dublin: printed by H Fitzpatrick, 1799. 86pp.

Date: 'This Day is published' (DJ 15/6/99 p. 3 col. 1).
Authorship: Theobald M'Kenna (title-page).

BLACK 2120

RIA: HT 329/6 • NLI: P 612/3
NLI: I 6551 Dublin (1799) 11 • KID: 1/2

second edition with additions and corrections. Dublin: printed by H Fitzpatrick, 1799. 88pp.

RIA: HP 786/ 5 • RIA: HT 310/1 • RIA: HT 315/3
RIA: HT 329/5 ('from the author', in orig. blue covers)
NLI: P 156/5 • BL: 8146 ee 23 (4)

third edition with additions and corrections. Dublin: printed by H Fitzpatrick, 1799. 86pp.

RIA: HT 311/19 • RIA: HT 330/2 • NLI: 128/2 • BL: 8146 bbb 11

C24 Constitutional strictures on particular positions advanced in the speeches of the right hon. William Pitt in the debates which took place between Great Britain and Ireland on the 23rd and 31st of January 1799. By Willoughby, earl of Abingdon. London: printed for T Barnes [1799]. 26pp.

Authorship: Willoughby Bertie (1740-1799), earl of Abingdon (title-page).

New Hampshire Hist Soc. : Y - King - 43

C25 A correspondence between two Milesian gentlemen on the affairs of the nation, to which is prefixed a long and very interesting dedication addressed to the noble peers of the quandam Irish parliament relative to their meritorious conduct on the great question of the union. [signed Vindex, prelims missing? in BL copy, 31pp. 21cm.]

BL: 1578/6513

D

D1 Dean Tucker's arguments on the propriety of an union between Great Britain and Ireland written some years since and now first published in this tract upon the same subject. By the rev. Dr Clarke. Dublin: printed for J Milliken, 1799. 64pp.

Date: advertised DJ 25/5/99 p. 2 col. 1.
Authorship: Josiah Tucker (1712-1799) and Thomas Brooke Clarke (title-page).

BLACK 2062   RIA: HP 786/2 • NLI: P 609/3
DCPL: 941.57/3 • RLM: PA 869/2

D2 {The union.} The debate in the House of Commons of Great Britain on the subject of an union with Ireland, to which is added the king's message and the proceedings of the Lords. Dublin: printed by J Moore, 1799. 38pp.

BLACK 2180   TCD: V h 25 (15) • TCD: 91 p. 13 (16) • RIA: HP 787/ 14
NLI: I 6551 Dublin (1799) 6 • NLI: P 620/12
BL: 1509/1140 • Bod: Vet A5 e 5296

D3 Debate in the House of Commons of Ireland on Wednesday the 15th of May 1799. Dublin: printed by J Moore, 1799. 58pp.

Date: 'No better proof can be given how sorely the Anti-Union Patriots feel the rebuke given by Lord Castlereagh to their Champion on the 15th of May, than the observation - that in their official account of that debate, as published by Mr James Moore, the Speech of Lord Castlereagh is contracted into a very brief summary of what he really delivered.' (DJ news item, 6/6/99 p. 3 col 3)

TCD: 91 p 13 (10) • TCD: 91 p 38 no. 13 • RIA: HP 786/ 7
RIA: HT 319/11 • RIA: HT 322/11 • NLI: P 617/4
BL: 287 g 14 (4) • CUL: Hib. 5. 799. 42

D4 Delectando pariterque monendo. [no imprint] single small sheet.

Note: A mock advertisement for 'a very ingenious glossary' and 'also, a most Learned Dissertation, in the true Shandean manner, upon co-partnership Productions of Genius and Public Addresses' - i.e. a squib aimed at pamphleteering, preserved in a volume otherwise wholly made up of anti-union material emanating in one form or another from Vincent Dowling. Thus it could be dated to c. 1799. But ESTC, recording only the TCD copy, dates it to c. 1770 without giving evidence. Reference to sansculottes make such a dating impossible.

TCD: S ee 55 (1)

D5 A demonstration of the necessity of a legislative union of Great Britain and Ireland involving a refutation of every argument which has been or can be urged against that measure. By a philosopher. Dublin: printed and sold by the booksellers, 1799. 40pp.

Authorship: attributed to 'Mr Holmes, tutor to Ld Charlemt' in TCD: Crofton 184 flyleaf list. Black gives Robert Holmes. RIA: HP 789/ 3 t-p ms. note attributes to Robert Holmes, esq.

BLACK 2098   TCD: V h 25 no. 7 • TCD: Crofton 184/3
                           TCD: Crofton 204/3 • TCD: Lecky A 4 34 no. 3
              RIA: HP 789/ 3 • RIA: HT 310/10 • NLI: P 107/13
        NLI: P 623/13 • BL: 8146 ee 23 (5) • Bod: G Pamphlets 243/8
  Bod: Vet A5 e 5213 • CUL: Hib. 5. 799. 160 • CUL: Hib 5 798. 68 (4)

Dublin: printed for James Moore, 1799. 40pp.

Date: 'just published' (DJ 10/1/99 p. 3 col. 4).

NLI: P 617/5 • NLI: I 6551 Dublin (1799) 5

D6 Detached thoughts on an union offered with all due respect to the Irish nation. By a citizen of Cork. Cork: printed by M Harris, 1799. 18pp.

BLACK 2073   NLI: JP 2225 • RLM: PA 35/15

D7 The doctrine of 'An appeal of the people and the 'Right of resistance' as laid down by Mr Saurin in the Irish House of Commons considered and confuted in a letter to a member of the Irish parliament. By the reverend Dr Clarke. London: printed for John Hatchard, 1800. 20pp.

Authorship: Thomas Brooke Clarke (p. 19). The BL copy was presented by the author to Sir Joseph Banks, that in RIA to [Alexander] 'Marsden Esq'.

RIA: HT 336/8 • BL: B 505 (8)

E

E1 English union is Ireland's ruin! Or an address to the Irish nation. By Hibernicus. Dublin: printed for James Moore, 1799. 32pp.

Authorship: attributed to 'Mr Boustead of Cork' in TCD: Crofton 185; to James Digges Latouche, by Black.

BLACK 2109   TCD: V h 23 no. 9 • TCD: Crofton 205/6 • RIA: HP 787/ 8
                  RIA: HT 324/8 • NLI: 622/2 • BL: 8145 de 11 (3)

E2 An epistle to Bonaparte from an anti-unionist. Dublin: printed for J Milliken,

1800. 8pp.

House of Lords Record Office P.T. vol 4 no 10 (Peel Tracts)

E3 The evidence of messrs Joshua Pim, John Orr, Thomas Abbot, Jacob Geoghegan, Leland Crosthwaite, Denis Thomas O'Brien, Harry Sadleir, John Duffy, Francis Kirkpatrick, John Anderson, Nicholas Grimshaw, James Dickey, John Houston, Daniel Dickinson, Thomas Blair, George Binns, John Locker, James Williams, and Thomas Kenny, as delivered before the committee of the whole House on his excellency the lord lieutenant's message respecting a legislative union with Great Britain. Cork: printed by James Haly, 1800. 36pp.

BLACK 2218   NLI: JP 386

E4 An examination into the origin and continuance of the discontents in Ireland and the true cause of the rebellion, being a faithful narrative of the particular sufferings of the Irish peasantry with a plan which, if adopted, cannot fail to bring back the Roman Catholic insurgents to their allegiance without injury to the protestant interest, or what they never asked, emancipation; to which is added a specimen of Irish anecdotes which the editor proposes on a future occasion to enlarge. By William Bingley. London: printed for and sold by the editor, 1799. x, [1], 4-50pp.
Date: date line January 1799 (p. x).

Authorship: William Bingley ('fourteen years a resident in Ireland' title-page).
Note: the text is very close to that of E-5 below which, however, advertises its libellous gossiping about Arthur Young's sex life on the title-page.

BL: 579 h 14 (2)

[same title, same imprint]. [4]pp.

Note: this is an advertising leaflet consisting of the prelims and final page of the substantive work; p. 46 is listed as providing 'A few words on the proposed union'.

Bod: G Pamphlets 2201/32

E5 An examination of the origin of the discontents in Ireland with remarks on the writings and interference ex officio of Arthur Young; being a faithful narrative of the particular sufferings of the Roman Catholic peasantry from the operation of tythes, the payment and exactions of surplice fees etc., shewing by a very easy method a plan for the tranquillization of that kingdom. By William Bingley. London: printed for and sold by the editor, 1799. x [1] 4-48pp.
Date: date line January 1799 (p. x).

Authorship: William Bingley ('fourteen years a resident in Ireland' title-page).

CUL: Hib 4. 799. 2 • Union Theological Seminary (N.Y.): LZ50 1799 pam

E6 An examination into the principles contained in a pamphlet entitled The speech of lord Minto, with some remarks upon a pamphlet entitled Observations on that part of the speaker's speech which relates to trade. By the right hon. Barry, earl Farnham. Dublin: printed for James Moore, 1800. 62pp.

Note: errata on p. 62.
Authorship: Barry Maxwell (d. 1800), 1st earl of Farnham - title-page.

BLACK 2221   RIA: HT 337/8 (incomplete, 66pp. only)
                    NLI: P 617/10 • NLI: P 1721 (14) • NLI: P 706/16

second edition. Dublin: printed for James Moore, 1800. 62pp.

Note: errata on p. 62, not identical to but overlapping with those in 1st ed.

        TCD: Lecky A 3 35 (unnumbered, between 7 & 8) • RIA: HT 337/6
        BL: 8145 dd 59 • CUL: Hib. 5. 800. 27 • CUL: Hib. 7. 800. 11

third edition. Dublin: printed for J Moore, 1800. 62pp.

                                                        BL: 1609/519

London: printed for G G & J Robinson by G Woodfall, 1800. 54pp.

                Free Library of Pennsylvania: London 1800 Examination

E7 An exposition of the principal terms of union and its probable effects on Ireland. Dublin: printed by J Milliken, 1800. 20pp.

BLACK 2219   RIA: HT 336/2 • NLI: P 617/11

E8 Extracts from de Foe's History of the union. Dublin: printed by John Exshaw, 1799. 68pp

                                    RIA: HT 330/7 • NLI: P 83/1

E9 Extracts from a narrative of the conversion of an Asian prince to the Christian faith, and letters on religious subjects. London: printed for W Flexney, [n.d.] 184pp.

Note: BL dates this rare item alternatively 1795? and 1799?: ESTC opts for 1798? If the later dating is accepted, then this constitutes an (unique?) instance, for the period under consideration, of the union's being discussed (pp. 169-174) in a work of fiction, albeit a tendentious one. But cf. C3 (*Castle Rackrent*) above, where union is linked by way of (extra-fictional?) comment to a novel.

                                                        BL: 1609/3547

F

F1 A fair representation of the present political state of Ireland, in a course of strictures on two pamphlets, one entitled The case of Ireland re-considered, the other entitled Considerations of the state of public affairs in the year 1799 - Ireland; with observations on other modern publications on the subject of an incorporating union of Great Britain and Ireland, particularly on a pamphlet entitled The speech of lord Minto in the House of Peers April 11 1799. By Patrick Duigenan. London: printed [by S Gosnell] for J Wright, 1799. 256pp. (inc ads.)

Date: In an elaborate three-part publicity campaign, readers of the Dublin Journal were progressively informed - 'Doctor Duigenan - a new work .. has just appeared in London ... Milliken is printing an Edition of this Work (DJ 12/11/99 p. 3 col 4.); 'in a few days will be published' (DJ 19/11/99 p. 3 col 4.); 'This Day is published' (DJ 30/11/99 p. 3 col 2.)
Authorship: Patrick Duigenan (1735-1816) - title page.

BLACK 2079   TCD: Lecky A 3 25 (3) • KID: 49/3 • BL: 8145 c 18
                                      RIA: HT 332/13 • Bod: G Pamphlets 618/5
                                Bod: G Pamphlets 915/4 • CUL: Hib. 7. 799. 8
                                                        CUL: Hib. 5. 799. 31

second edition. London: printed [by S Gosnell] for J Wright, 1799. 256pp. (inc. ads)

                              BL: 1103 g 6 (2) • Bod: G Pamphlets 1205/7

third edition. London: printed [by S Gosnell] for J Wright, 1800. 256pp. (inc ads.)

                                                        RLM: PA 1127/2

Dublin: printed for J Milliken, 1800. 260pp.

                                                        BLACK 2213

Genuine edition corrected by the author. Dublin: printed for J Milliken, 1800. 254pp.

                              RIA: HP 805/6 • BL: 1490 p 118 • CUL: Hib. 5. 800. 22
                                                        CUL: Hib. 5. 800. 23

F2 A few observations accounting for the apparent apathy that has prevailed on the question of union. Dublin: printed by J Stockdale, 1800. 16pp.

Authorship: Signs off, p. 16, An Irishman.

                    TCD: Crofton 208/7 • RIA: HT 336/11 • NLI: P 622/9

F3 A few thoughts on an union with some observations on Mr Weld's pamphlet of "No union", addressed to the yeomenry [sic] of Dublin. By a wellwisher of

Ireland. Dublin: printed for J Milliken, 1799. 38pp.

Date: listed in Milliken's advert. DJ 29/1/99 p. 4 col 4.
Authorship: attributed to 'Alexr Tytler esq' in TCD: Crofton 184 fly-leaf list.

BLACK 2083   TCD: V h 24 no. 14 • TCD: Crofton 184/10
                        TCD: Crofton 204/11 • TCD: Lecky A 4 34 no. 11
                    RIA: HT 310/20 • RIA: HT 321/6 • RIA: HT 327/8
                                        BL: 111 e 2 • BL: 117 h 37

F4 A few words in favour of Ireland by way of reply to a pamphlet called "An impartial view of the causes leading this country to the necessity of an union". By no lawyer. Dublin: printed and sold by the book-sellers, 1799. 36pp.

Authorship: ESTC attributes this to Thomas Grady.

                                        NLI: JP 575 • RIA: HT 321/11

F5 First letter to a noble lord on the subject of the union. By Giles S Smyth. Dublin: printed for J Moore, 1799. 34pp.

Date: a title-page ms. note on RIA: HP 766/16 (a copy of the 2nd ed.) reads '1st Ed. 1798'.
Authorship: Giles S Smyth (title-page).

BLACK 2166   TCD: Crofton 212/4 (original state) • RIA: HT 328/10
                                            NLI: P 251/14

second edition. Dublin: printed by J Moore, 1799. 34pp.

            TCD: V h 21 no. 13 • TCD: Crofton 182/11 • TCD: Crofton 202/10
                TCD: Lecky A 4 32 no. 14 • RIA: HP 766/16 • RIA: HT 318/10
                        RIA: HT 325/4 • RIA: HT 333/1 • NLI: P 2/11
                    NLI: I 6551 Dublin (1799) 23 • BL: 8145 de 11 (6)
                        Bod: Vet A5 e 5258 • CUL: Hib. 7. 799. 47

F6 Free thoughts on the misconception of the superiority of natural advantages possessed by this country over England. Dublin: printed for James Moore, 1799. 14pp.

Authorship: signs off, p. 14, Verax.

BLACK 2088   TCD: Crofton 205/9 • RIA: HP 787/ 11 • BL: 8146 f 34 (14)

Dublin: printed for James Moore, 1799. 16pp.

Authorship: no implied author's name on p. 14.

                                TCD: 91 p 38 no. 1 • RIA: HT 332/19

F7 The friends of an union the enemies of Ireland. Cork: printed by J Connor, 1798. 32pp.

BLACK 2006   NLI: I 6551 Cork 1798 • RIA: HT 306/9 • BL: 8132 ee 5 (4)

G

G1 The glass inverted; or, another view of the times. Dublin: printed for J Milliken, 1799. 20pp.

Note: in verse: see pp. 9, 18-19 re union.

TCD: Crofton 142/ 8 • NLI: P 777/1

G2 The good old castle on the rock: or union the one thing needful, addressed to the people of England. Third edition. London: printed for J Wright, 1798. 24pp.

Authorship: a work called The castle on the rock is attributed to A. Kendall in the NLI Dix Catalogue of provincial Irish printings (see under Cork).

Note: This is so vapid a composition that the identification of its topic is almost impossible, the union seems to be implicated as just one of many sorts of coming together required in revolutionary times.

BL: 8132 de 3 (8)

G3 The great Mrs Britain's second benefit, amphitheatre, near the College-Square on Wednesday February 12 will be performed an entirely new politico-dramatic olio called Self-immolation, or the wise men of Gotham. [Dublin, 1800] s sh fol

Note: CUL: Hib. o. 800. 4 carries ms. identifications of notables with disreputable parts in the mock-drama.

TCD: S ee 55 (3) • BL: 1325 g 15 (2) • CUL: Hib. o. 800. 2
CUL: Hib. o. 800. 4

H

H1 An hasty sketch of Mr Pitt's celebrated administration, most respectfully inscribed to the right honourable Lord Auckland. London: printed for the author by S Gosnell, 1800. 78pp.

Authorship and date: Joseph Cawthorne - signed p. 57 with date-line 'Greenwich Park, written in the year 1797'; pp. 59-78 are 'Appendix written in 1800'.
Note: The BL copy title-page bears the ms inscription 'This pamphlet will not be published without permission.' The text is much given over to an attack on 'the celebrated and *busy* Earl of Shelburne of the kingdom of Ireland ...' (p. 7) ... 'this Irish Prime Minister of Great Britain [who] separated thirteen colonies from the crown of Great Britain for ever. The glory of such a *separation* is more congenial to the Irish than the English character, which would more naturally glory in a valuable *acquisition*.' (p. 9) See also p. 65 re Ireland.

H2 Hear him! hear him! in a letter to the right hon. John Foster. By Theophilus Swift. Dublin: printed by J Stockdale, 1799. 66pp.

Date: date-line, p. 66, Drumcondra August 27 1799.
Authorship: Theophilus Swift - title-page.

BLACK 2169   TCD: Crofton 206/7 • RIA: HP 786/ 10 • RIA: HT 310/2
                              BL: 8146 bbb 23 (3) • CUL: Hib. 5. 798. 68 (19)

H3 Hem! Hip! Hollo! Dont be alarmed. The Pimlico parliamentary register no 1 .... taken in short hand by Posthumous Stenographicus Woodfall esq. London: (n.p.n.d.)

Date: ms note in BL suggests 1808 as date of publication.

BL: 1325 g 15 (12)

H4 A hint concerning the causes that may have encouraged the English minister to entertain that extraordinary project of a union. Dublin: printed for V Dowling, 1800. 14pp.

NLI: P 2/8

second edition. Dublin: printed for Vincent Dowling, 1800. 14pp.

RIA: HT 336/3

H5 A hint to the inhabitants of Ireland. By a native. Dublin: [n p], 1800. 12pp.

Date: date-line: February 1800 (p. 11)
Authorship: on the collective title-page of Tracts .. on the union vol 8 (see TCD: Crofton 209) this item, is listed on the same line as An appeal to the loyal citizens of Dublin (A21 above) which may be by Thomas Lewis O'Beirne. A hint ... is not included in Crofton 209.

BLACK 2234   TCD: Lecky A 3 35 (7) • BL: 1609/3996
                                                  CUL: Hib. 5. 798. 68 (12)

H6 Hints to the people especially to the inhabitants of Dublin, in which the effects of an union on the trade and property of Dublin are investigated. By William Stevens. Dublin: printed by H Fitzpatrick, 1799. 32pp.

Date: 'on Monday next will be Published' , ie on 22/1/99 (DJ 19/1/99 p. 3 col 4).
Authorship: William Stevens (title-page); RIA: HT 328/7 blue top cover in holograph gives name as 'Stephens'.

BLACK 2167   TCD: V h 24 no. 5 • RIA: HT 328/7

H7 An historical deduction of an union between Great Britain and Ireland. Dublin: printed by Robert Napper for Bennett Dugdale, 1799. 32pp.

Date: date line, p. 31, Dublin January 15 1799; 'just published ... by B. Dugdale, Bookseller ...' (DJ 17/1/99 p. 4 col. 4)

TCD: Crofton 202/13 • RIA: HT 321/10 • BL: 8145 de 8 (2)

H8 The history of the union between England and Scotland, to which is added the articles of union etc. By Daniel de Foe. Dublin: printed by John Exshaw, 1799. 214pp.

Authorship: Daniel Defoe (1661?-1731) - title-page.
Date: Exshaw twice advertised a work similarly named:
   In DJ 24/12/98 he announced 'Just imported ... a Few Copies Price £1 18s in Boards'. These were probably copies of a truncated version of the original (1709) text with some new matter, first published by Stockdale of London in 1786 and re-issued by him in 1795 with the title-page date unaltered. (Stockdale's subtitle read '...with an introduction in which the consequences and probability of a like union between this country and Ireland are considered.' This was 'An essay containing a few strictures on the union of Scotland with England and on the present situation of Ireland, being an introduction to de Foe's history of the union, by J. L. de Lorme' (pp. 1-96, separately paginated and with title-page dated 1787 [sic].
   In DJ 22/1/99, Exshaw announced 'This Day is Published by John Exshaw .. price 4s 4d' (p. 2 col. 2). In neither advertisement is the book title as give on the title-page of the copies inspected and listed below - both advertised titles being a great deal longer. This 1799 edition contains only three sections of the original (1709) text.

BLACK 2072   TCD: Crofton 210/4 • RIA: HT 310/6 • RIA: HT 321/2
                    RIA: HT 314/1 • RIA: HT 333/2 • BL: 8142 d 8

H9 The history of the union of Scotland and England stating the circumstances which brought that event forward to a conclusion, and the advantages resulting from it to the Scots. By the rev. Ebeneezer Marshal. Edinburgh: printed for Peter Hill, and Longman & Rees [London], 1799. 260pp.

Authorship: Ebeneezer Marshal (d. 1813) - title-page.

BL: 601 e 11/2 • BL: 601 e 14

H10 The hunt in Ireland. By a member of parliament. Dublin: printed and sold by the book-sellers, 1799. 16pp.

Note: in verse.

NLI: I 6551 Dublin (1799) 16

I

I1 Impartial remarks on the subject of an union in answer to arguments in favour of that measure in which the sentiments of the Catholic body are vindicated from the charge of favouring the project with a reply to Mr McKenna's Memoire. By a farmer. Dublin: printed for William Jones, 1799. 48pp.

Date: 'This Day is published' (DJ 19/1/99 p. 3 col. 4)

BLACK 2100   TCD: V h 24 no. 16 • TCD: Crofton 204/14
                          RIA: HP 789 /10 • RIA: HT 323/11 • RIA: HT 327/11
                          NLI: 621/10 • BL: 8146 f 34 (13)

I2 An impartial view of the causes leading this country to the necessity of an
union; in which the two leading characters of the state are contrasted; and in
which is contained a reply to Cease your funning and Mr Jebb. Dublin: printed
for Bernard Dornin, 1799. 54pp.

Date: Date-line, p. 53, 4th Jan. 1799. 'This Day was Published' (DJ 5/1/99 p. 3 col. 1)

BLACK 2101   RIA: HP 767/17 • RIA: HT 319/7
                          RIA: HT 310/19 (final leaf damaged)
                          NLI: JP 3356 • CUL: Hib. 5. 799. 43

I3 An impartial view of the causes leading this country to the necessity of an
union; in which the two leading characters of the state are contrasted; and in which
is contained a history of the rise and progress of Orange men; a reply to Cease your
funning, and Mr Jebb. Third edition. Dublin: printed for B Dornin, 1799. 54pp.

Date: Date-line (p. 53) Dublin 4th Jan. 1799; 'This Day is Published' (DJ 15/1/99 p. 1
col. 3)
Print run: 'One thousand copies sold in four days' (DJ 15/1/99 p. 1 col. 3)

                TCD: V h 23 no. 2 • TCD: Lecky A 4 33 no. 16 • RIA: HT 319/8
          NLI: P 617/12 • RLM: PA753/2 • BL: 1508/839 • BL: 1508/1561
                          Bod: 226 i 464

I4 The interests and present state of the nation considered with thoughts on the
British connexion. By a barrister. Dublin: printed by J Rice, 1797. 62pp.

Note: Principally an attack on Grattan, conducted in the cause of 'national concurrence'
between Britain and Ireland; p. 61 concludes 'end of the first part'.

                                        CUL: Hib. 7. 797. 6

I5 An investigation of the legality and validity of a union. By John Bernard
Trotter. Dublin: printed by H Fitzpatrick, 1799. 42pp.

Authorship: John Bernard Trotter - title-page.

BLACK 2176   TCD: V h 23 no. 4 • RIA: HP 787/ 3 • RIA: HT 328/3
                          NLI: P 615/12 • BL: 8145 cc 105

I6 Ireland profiting by example, or the question whether Scotland has gained or
lost by an union with England fairly discussed in a letter from a gentleman in
Edinburgh to his friend in Dublin. Dublin: printed for J Milliken, 1799. 36pp.

Date: Listed in Milliken advertisement DJ 29/1/99 p. 4 col 6.
Authorship and print run: Alexander Fraser Tytler, lord Woodhouselee (1747-1813) - see

Archibald Alison's Memoir in *Trans. Roy. Soc. of Edinburgh* vol 8 (1818) esp. pp. 551-2 where it is claimed that 'such was its merit, or its popularity, that three thousand copies were sold upon the day of its publication.' Attributed to 'Alexr Tytler esq' in TCD: Crofton 184 fly-leaf list. BL cataloque gives 'Colonel Tittler'. Black concurs.

BLACK 2173   TCD: V h 24 no. 10 • TCD: Lecky A 4 34 no. 9
RIA: HP 789/ 6 • RIA: HT 323/ 13 • RIA: HT 328/8
NLI: P 617/13 • NLI: 622/1 • BL: 117 h 13
BL: 1600/1315 • Bod: Vet A5 e 5214

third edition. Dublin: printed for J Milliken, 1799. 32pp.

TCD: Crofton 184/8 • TCD: Crofton 204/9 • RIA: HT 317/9
BL: 8146 f 34 (10)

London: printed by J Plymsell at the Anti-Jacobin press, [n.d.] 32pp.

Date: title-page of RIA: 797/12 carries ms date '1800'.

RIA: HP 797/12 • BL: 111 d 46

I7 Ireland sabinized; or, a case in point. Dublin: pritned [sic] by J Hill, 1799. 16pp.

Date: the original blue paper covers of RIA: HT 321/13 bear the ms title and the date '10 Jany 1799'.

TCD: V h 23 no. 13 • TCD: Lecky A 4 33 no. 15 • TCD: 91 p 38 no. 7
RIA: HP 767/ 16 • RIA: HT 321/13 • NLI: I 6551 Dublin (1799) 53
BL: 8145 de 12 (6)

I8 Irish independence or the policy of union. Dublin: printed by J Milliken, 1800. 82pp.

BLACK 2236   TCD: Lecky A 3 35 (6) • TCD: Crofton 208/5
RIA: HT 339/4 (authorial ms. note on t-p) • NLI: P 226/8
NLI: P 617/14 • BL: 1609/518 • CUL: Hib. 5. 800. 42

I9 Irish salvation promulged, or the effects of an union with Great Britain candidly investigated in an evening's conversation between a farmer and school-master. By William Percy. Belfast: [pr]inted by J Smyth, 1800. 24pp.

Date-line (p. iv) - Comber 4 May 1800.
Authorship: William Percy (1771-) - title-page.

BLACK 2255   RIA: HP 797/10 • NLI: P 613/12 • NLI: P 617/9 (incomplete)

K

K1 Keep up your spirits, or huzza for the empire!! being a fair, argumentative defence of an union addressed to the people of Ireland. By a citizen of the Isle of

Man. Dublin: printed for J Moore, 1799. 28pp.

Date: 'Just published' (DJ 10/1/99 p. 3 col 4)

BLACK 2106   TCD: V h 23 no. 6 • TCD: Lecky A 4 33 no. 17
          TCD: Crofton 203/10 • TCD: 91 p 38 no. 2 • RIA: HP 767/18
                              RIA: HT 328/1 • NLI: Ir 94107 t 3 (2.18)
                                  BL: 1608/2789 • BL: 8145 de 10 (6)

L

L1 The last speech and dying words, with the birth, parentage, education, life, character and behaviour of that notorious and flagitious British Impostor known by the nickname of the sun who was burnt at the stake by the hands of the common hangman in College-Green Dublin on Monday the 11th of February 1799 for perpetrating a false, slanderous and daring attack upon the House of Commons of Ireland, who rescued their country from a project more odious than the deadly plot of Titus Oates namely the treacherous measure of an union. Dublin: printed at the Sun-fire Office by O'Donnel and Co., [bogus imprint, 1799] s. sh fol.

Note: The word sun appears in an eight-pointed star, with the motto *Lucus a non Lucendo* appended; cf Byron's speech on Catholic Emancipation in the British House of Lords where the same obscure Latin adage is deployed to mock the union (*Debate in Both Houses of Parliament, in April 1812, on Motions Made by the Earl of Donoughmore and the Right Hon. Henry Grattan, for a Committee to Inquire into the State of the Laws Imposing Civil Disability on his Majesty's Roman Catholic Subjects* (London: W Smith, [1812], pp. 109-10.)

          TCD: S ee 55 (6) • BL: 1325 g 15 (4) • Bod: G Pamphlets 2201/31

L2 Legal arguments occasioned by the project between Great Britain and Ireland on the exclusion, on the exclusion of the Roman Catholic nobility and gentry in both kingdoms from parliament. By a member of the honourable society of Lincoln's Inn. London: for the author, 1799. 58pp.

Authorship: attributed to Sir John Joseph Dillon in Goldsmiths Cat.

                    BL: 701 e 17 (5) • BL: 111 d 63 • BL: 117 h 36
                    CUL: Hib. 5. 799. 53 • CUL: Hib. 5. 799. 54

Dublin: printed from the author's edition published in London, by H Fitzpatrick, 1799. 40pp.

Date: 'This Day is published (DJ 15/6/99 p. 3).

    RIA: HT 326/10 • NLI: P 112/6 • BL: 1560/1146 • Bod: Vet A5 e 5292

L3 A letter addressed to a gentleman in England considering the principal arguments against an union and deciding in favour of the measure. Dublin:

printed by H Fitzpatrick, 1799. 52pp.

Date: Date line, p. 51, January 18 1799. 'This Day is Published' (DJ 22/1/99 p. 4 col. 2).

BLACK 2111   TCD: V h 24 no. 3 • RIA: HT 321/2 • RIA: HT 330/10
                                         NLI: P 618/3 • BL: 8145 cc 74

L4 A letter addressed to the gentlemen of England and Ireland on the inexpediency of a federal-union between the two kingdoms. By Sir John J W Jervis. Dublin: printed by John Whitworth, 1798. 72pp.

Date-line, p. 71, 15 Dec 1798; in RIA: HP 766/ 7 a T-p ms. note reads '14 Decr 1798'. Authorship: John Jervis White Jervis (1766-1830, 1st baronet) - title-page. Note: errata p. [72].

BLACK 2012 TCD: V h 22 no. 1 • TCD: Crofton 182/9 • TCD: Crofton 202/8
                    TCD: Lecky A 4 32 no. 12 • NLI: P 211/2 • NLI: P 251/16
                            RIA: HP 766/ 7 • BL: 8145 de 12 (8)

[London:] Dublin printed; London reprinted for J Debrett, 1798. 72pp.

                              CUL: Hib. 5. 798. 36 • CUL: Hib. 7. 798. 10

L5 A letter from Ben. Bousfield esq. to the citizens of Cork. Cork: printed by James Haly, 1799. 32pp.

Authorship: Benjamin Bousfield - title-page.

BLACK 2054   RIA: HT 318/8 • NLI: JP 5131

second edition. Cork: printed by James Haly, 1799. 32pp.

                    TCD: V h 25 no. 16 • TCD: 91 p 13 (5) • RIA: HT 331/1
                            NLI: I 6551 Cork 1799 • BL: 8145 cc 8

L6 A letter from Darby Tracy, chairman in London, to Mr Denis Feagan, breeches-maker at Edenderry, wherein is clearly proved the effeccts which an union with Great Britain will have on the interest and happiness of the common people of Ireland. Dublin: printed by W Folds, 1799. 16pp.

BLACK 2175   RIA: HT 315/14 • RIA: HT 316/13 • NLI: JP 578
                            NLI: P 615/11 • Bod: Vet A5 e 3418/1

second edition. Dublin: printed by W Folds, 1799. 16pp.

                                                  BL: 8145 dd 72

third edition. Dublin: printed by W Folds, 1799. 16pp.

                                                  BL: 1609/511

L7 A letter from Murtagh Feagan cousin german to Denis Feagan of Edenderry in answer to Darby Tracy of London, chairman, srewing [sic] (nothing but truth). Dublin: printed by J Stockdale, 1800. 8pp.

Date and Authorship: signs off p. 8 with the supposed author's name + his mark, date line Edenderry 22d Dec. 1799.
Note: copies with the correct spelling of 'shewing' also exist - e.g. the CUL copy listed.

BLACK 2222   RIA: HT 335/23 • RIA: HT 337/10 • BL: 8146 c 23
                                            CUL: Hib. 5. 798. 68 (13)

L8 Letter from a retired barrister in London to a practicing barrister in Dublin. Dublin: printed for J Milliken, 1799. 28pp.

(Date line, p. 27, London, December the 29th 1798)
Authorship: attributed to 'Alexr Marsden esq' in TCD: Crofton 184 fly-leaf list.

BLACK 2112   TCD: V h 24 no. 15 • TCD: Crofton 184/7
                        TCD: Crofton 204/7 • TCD: Lecky A 4 34 no. 7
                    RIA: HP 789/4 • RIA: HT 317/3 • RIA: HT 323/12
            RIA: HT 331/5 • BL: 8146 f 34 (11) • Bod: G Pamphlets 243/2

L9 A letter from Rusticus to a young member of the Irish House of Commons. Cork: printed by James Haly, 1800. 24pp.

Authorship: Black gives 'Boustead, -?' citing no evidence.

BLACK 2197   RIA: HT 335/2 • KID: 50/5 • BL: 1609/513

L10 A letter to the electors of Ireland on the projected measure of an union, with some friendly hints to the borough patrons of Ireland. By a freeholder. Dublin: printed for J Moore, 1799. 16pp.

Authorship: attributed by implication to 'Mr Spencer' [ie Joshua Spencer] in ms note in TCD: Crofton 185.

BLACK 2114   TCD: Crofton: 185/ 1 • TCD: Crofton 212/3
                                RLM: PA 867/2 • BL: 8145 de 8 (6)

[same imprint] 18pp.

Note: errata p. 17.

                        TCD: V h 22 no. 14 • RIA: HP 787/ 1 • NLI: P 621/12
                                KID: 43/14 • BL: 8146 ee 23 (9)

L11 A letter to the farmers & [sic] traders of Ireland on the subject of union. May 1st 1800. By a farmer and trader. Dublin: printed for the author, 1800. 20pp.

Note: A ms note on p. 19 of the NLI copy reads 'this was written to soften a bad mea[sure] and to reconcile a bad-bargain [sic] S'

BLACK 2242   RIA: HP 797/11 • RIA: HT 336/4 • NLI: 125/2

RLM: PA 753/6

and [sic] traders of Ireland on the subject of union. May 1st. 1800. By a farmer and trader. Dublin printed; London: reprinted for J and T Carpenter, 1800. 20pp.

Note: printed by S Gosnell, Little Queen Street, Holborn, (p. 19).

BL: 8145 c 39

L12 A letter to his excellency marquis Cornwallis on the proposed union in which his excellency's political situation is candidly discussed. By an Irishman. Dublin: printed by James Moore, 1798. 40pp.

Authorship: attributed to 'Mr Ormsby' in Crofton 182 fly-leaf list.

BLACK 2018   TCD: V h 22 no. 8 • TCD: Crofton 182/12
TCD: 91 p 38 no. 3 • TCD: Lecky A 4 32 no. 15
RIA: HP 766/ 12 • RIA: HT 303/6 • RIA: HT 307/12
NLI: P 2/12 • NLI: P 221/3 • BL: 8145 de 11 (5)

L13 Letter to Henry Grattan esq MP etc etc. By William Smith. Dublin: printed by Marchbank, 1800. 134pp.

Authorship: [Sir] William Cusack Smith (1766-1836, 2nd baronet) - title-page.

RIA: HT 340/4 • NLI: P 226/6

third edition. Dublin: printed and sold by Marchbank, 1800. 156pp.

TCD: Crofton 208/9 • RIA: HT 335/3

third edition. Dublin: printed and sold by Marchbank, 1800. 96pp.

TCD: Lecky A 3 35 (9) • RIA: HT 337/12 • BL: 8145 d 68

L14 A letter to the Irish parliament on the intended bill for legalizing military law. Dublin: printed and sold by the book-sellers, 1799. 16pp.

Bod: G Pamphlets 243/9 • CUL: Hib. 5. 798. 68 (9)

L15 Letter to Joshua Spencer, esq. occasioned by his Thoughts on an union. By a barrister. Dublin: printed for John Archer, 1798. 42pp.

Date: ms note on the title-page of RIA: HP 766/4 reads 'published 8 Decr.'.
Authorship: William Johnson (1760-1845) - other edition.
Note: A variant has 'it is' (top of p. 9) in roman instead of italics , e.g. BL: 8145 d 4.

BLACK 2013   TCD: V h 21 no. 3 • TCD: Crofton 202/3
TCD: Lecky A 4 32 no. 4 • RIA: HP 766/4 • RIA: HT 305/6
NLI: P 221/6 • NLI: P 251/3 • NLI: Ir 94107 p 14 (3)
BL: 8145 d 4 • Bod: G pamphlets 1965/7

Cork: printed by J Haly, M Harris, and J Connor, 1798. 18pp.

RLM: PA 35/12

L16 A letter to Joshua Spencer esq on an union. Br Wm Johnson. Dublin printed; London: re-printed for Hatchard [et al], [1798.] 24pp.

Authorship: William Johnson - title-page.

TCD: Crofton 182/3 • BL: B 505 (10) • BL: 117 h 12
CUL: Hib. 5. 798. 37 • CUL: Hib. 5. 798. 61

L17 A letter to the king on behalf of the Irish nation with observations on the evil consequences of an union as destructive of the ballance [sic] of power within the state. By Hibernicus. Dublin: printed for Vincent Dowling, 1800. 40pp.

RIA: HT 336/14 • NLI: P 2/15 • NLI: P 622/3 • CUL: Hib. 5. 800. 36

L18 A letter to a noble lord containing a full declaration of the Catholic sentiment on the important question of union. By an Irish Catholic. Dublin: printed by G Folingsby, 1800. 8pp.

KID: 50/1

L19 Letter to the people of Ireland from E - M - esq on the advantages that would arise from an union with this country upon fair and equitable principles. London: printed by A Paris and sold by J St John, 1798. 30pp.

Duke Univ. (Perkins Library) : RBR E no. 636 v 2-2

L20 A letter to the people of Ireland which they can all understand and ought to read. By a real friend. Dublin: printed for J Milliken, 1799. 34pp.

Date: 'just published' (DJ 20/7/99 p. 3 col 4)

BLACK 2115   TCD: OLS 187 r 6 (5) • RIA: HP 786/ 8 • RIA: HT 322/12
RIA: HT 330/11 • NLI: I 6551 Dublin (1799) 18
BL: 8146 ee 23 (8)

[same imprint] 24pp.

NLI: P 212/12

L21 A letter to the right honorable John Foster. Dublin: printed in the year 1799. 20pp.

NLI: I 6551 Dublin (1799) 58

L22 A letter to the right honorable William Pitt. Dublin: printed by James

Moore, 1799. 48pp.

Date: date line 19th January 1799; a news item in DJ 13/8/99 (p. 3 col. 4) cites a hostile review of a 3rd edition of this title from the *British Critic* of July 1799. No 3rd ed. is listed below.
Authorship: William Drennan (p. 48).

BLACK 2077   TCD: V h 24 no. 8 • TCD: Crofton 182/15
                              TCD: Crofton 202/12 • TCD: Crofton 204/15
          TCD: Lecky A 4 34 no. 15 • TCD: 91 p 38 no. 16 • RIA: HP 789 /12
                    RIA: HT 310/10 • RIA: HT 326/11 • NLI: P 112/8
          NLI: 212/2 • NLI: P 221/15 • NLI: P 609/9 • BL: 8135 e 31
                                        Bod: G Pamphlets 243/7

[London:] Dublin: printed by James Moore; London: re-printed for G G and J Robinson, 1799. 48pp.

                                                        NLI: P 107/5

L23 A letter to Sir John Newport bart on the expediency of a legislative union between Great and Ireland. By William Hughes. London: printed by M Allen, 1799. 50pp.

Authorship: William Hughes (title-page).

                    Univ. of Kansas (Spencer Research Lib.): C5770 item 6

L24 A letter to Theobald M'Kenna esq, the Catholic advocate, in reply to the calumnies against the Orange Institution contained in his pamphlet purporting to be a Memoire on some questions respecting the projected union etc etc etc, with observations on the new and further claims of the Catholics as affecting the constitution and protestant establishment, with an appendix containing some animadversions on the popular pamphlet entitled An important view of the causes leading this country to the necessity of an union" etc ec etc. By an Orangeman. Dublin: printed for J Milliken, 1799. 36pp.

(Date line, p. 35, January 22 1799)

      TCD: V h 24 no. 12 • TCD: Lecky A 4 33 no. 6 • TCD: Crofton 203/5
          RIA: HP 780/ 7 • RIA: HT 333/5 • NLI: P 623/11 • BL: 1509/1159

L25 A letter to Theobald M'Kenna esq. occasioned by a publication entitled A memoire on some questions respecting the projected union. By John Hamilton. Dublin: printed by James Moore, 1799. 64pp.

Date: 'Just published' (DJ 10/1/99 p. 3 col. 4).
Authorship: John Hamilton (title-page).

BLACK 2095   TCD: V h 23 no. 8 (pp [61-62] blank: [63] type: [64] blank.)
                    TCD: Crofton 184/2 (as above) • TCD: Crofton 204/ 2
                              (appears to lack a leaf without loss of text)

TCD: Lecky A 4 34 no. 2 (as above)
RIA: HP 789/ 2 (lacks pp. [63-4].) • NLI: - P 612/2
BL: 1509/1171 Bod: Vet A5 e 5212

L26 A letter to William Smith esq. in answer to his Address to the people of Ireland in which his assertion of an absolute despotic power being acknowledged by our constitution is particularly examined. By one of the people. Dublin: printed by James Moore, 1799. 38pp.

Authorship: attributed to Charles Kendal Bushe in ms note in TCD: Crofton 185.

BLACK 2117   TCD: V h 25 no. 12 • TCD: Crofton 205/11
RIA: HT 324/14 • NLI: P 633/10 • BL: 8145 d 68

L27 Letters from a gentleman in Ireland to his friend at Bath. Cork: printed at the Herald-office, 1798. 42pp.

Authorship: Horace Townsend, see NLI Dix catalogue of provincial printing.

RIA: HP 745/4 • NLI: I 6551 Cork 1798 (15)

L28 Letters on the subject of union addressed to messrs Saurin and Jebb in which Mr Jebb's "Reply" is considered. By a barrister. Dublin: printed by J Milliken, 1799. 8opp.

Date: 'This Day is published ... "Six Letters ..." ' (DJ 8/1/99 p. 2 col. 4).
Authorship: Sir William Cusack Smith - BL and TCD. The RLM copy bears ms annotation in the first page of text, 'Right Honble Thomas Pelham from the Author', and the name William Smith written in over A barrister on the title-page, probably in the same hand.

BLACK 2163   TCD: V h 23 no. 16 • TCD: Lecky A 4 34 no. 4
TCD: Crofton 184/4 • TCD: Crofton 204/4 • RIA: HT 310/14
RIA: HT 322/3 • NLI: P 618/5 • RLM: PA 395/1
BL: 1103 g 10 (1) • BL: 117 h 17

L29 Letters on the subject of union in which Mr Jebb's Reply is considered, and the competence of parliament to bind Ireland to an union is asserted. By a barrister and member of parliament. [London:] Dublin printed; London re-printed for J Wright, 1799. 116pp.

CUL: Hib. 5. 799. 56 • CUL: Hib. 5. 799. 22 • CUL: Hib. 5. 798. 3/4

L30 List of the members of both houses of the Irish parliament who voted on a motion for an address to his majesty acceding to the discussion of a plan for a legislative union with Great Britain on the ever memorable 23d and 25th January 1799. Dublin: printed by V Dowling, 1799. single sheet, with engraving of John Foster in the centre.

Date: 'This Day published' (DJ 28/2/99 p. 3 col. 4)

TCD: S ee 55) • UCD : 26 1 17/1 • CUL: Hib. o. 799. 1

L31 A list of union pamphlets published by Milliken [Dublin: printed for J Milliken, 1799] 4pp.

Note: 17 items in favour of, and 32 items against, the union.

RIA: HT 333/5 (bound after) • BL: 1509/1173 (2)

L32 A loyal subject's thoughts on an union between Great Britain and Ireland. Dublin: printed for J Milliken, 1799. 38pp.

Date: Listed in Milliken advertisement, DJ 29/1/99 (p. 4 col. 4).

BLACK 2118   TCD: V h 24 no. 11 • TCD: Crofton 204/12
                                    TCD: Lecky A 4 34 no. 12 • RIA: HP 789/ 5
               RIA: HT 323/17 • NLI: P 112/3 • NLI: 618/7 • BL: 8146 f 34 (5)

M

M1 The mad music master, or union no harmony. [no imprint or date, c. 1800] single sheet print (coloured) with 12 lines of printed text.

TCD: Lecky A 7 38 (item 1, unnumbered)

M2 {Ireland} The means of restoring and preserving the tranquillity of Ireland. London: printed for the author and sold by J Parsons, 1798. 164pp.

Date-lines - July 16 1798 (p. 58); Aug 3 1798 (p. 103); Oct 17 1798 (p. 163). Address given as Greenwich Park.
Authorship: attributed to Joseph Cawthorne in TCD. Writer claims *The Crisis* ('thirteen years ago') on p. 29 and quotes from it extensively (pp. 33-51). Re union see pp. 23-27.

TCD: OLS L - 2- 43 (2)

M3 The measure of an incorporative legislative union considered with reference to the adjustment of 1782, with a modifying proposition addressed to every dispassionate loyal man of every order, sect, and persuasion in both kingdoms. By a member of the Irish legislature. Dublin: printed by R Marchbank, 1800. 12pp.

Authorship: t-p ms note on RIA copy attributes this to the earl of Bellermont, i. e. Charles Coote.

RIA: HT 336/9 • NLI: P 623/2

third edition. Dublin: printed by R Marchbank, 1800. 12pp.

BL: 8145 cc 79

M4 The melancholy consequences of a union displayed in a series of letters originally addressed to the right honourable the lord chancellor of Ireland. By

Marcus Curtius. London: printed for J Wright, 1799. 84pp.

Date: The eight letters are dated in October 1798; the advertisment (p. [ii]) refers to delay in publication due to 'an unforeseen accident which befel the Manuscript'.
Authorship: refers (p. 2) to himself as 'a native of the same country - a member of the same university' as Lord Clare (to whom the letters are nominally addressed), and explains his use of 'the name of a man, whose patriotism, at the instant expense of his life, once closed the gap that threatened to destroy his country' (p. 6). These details might, of course, be regarded as part of a fictitious 'persona'. Attributed to 'Doctor Burrowes' in ms note in TCD: Crofton 185, which may indicate Robert Burrowes (c. 1758-1841) a fellow of TCD, or (less likely) his brother Peter Burrowes (1753-1841), a radical lawyer. Despite the letters being addressed to Clare, the book is dedicated to Lords Enniskillen and Kingsborough, both of whom had been involved in scandals of one kind or another: the dedication might also be regarded as part of a fictional/satirical device.
Note: also issued with an errata leaf before the text, see copy in University College, Dublin.

BLACK 2071   TCD: Crofton 205/10 • RIA: HT 324/13 • NLI: P 401/10
                                     NLI: P 623/1 • RLM: 867/ 6

M5 A memoire on some questions respecting the projected union of Great Britain and Ireland. By Theobald M'Kenna. Dublin: printed for John Rice, 1799. 42pp.

Date: 'This Day is Published' (DJ 22/12/98 p. 3 col. 1).
Authorship: Theobald M'Kenna (title-page).

BLACK 2121   TCD: V h 22 no. 4 • TCD: Lecky A 4 33 no. 4
                                 TCD: Crofton 203/4 • RIA: HP 767/ 9
          RIA: (bound with) HT 303/15 • RIA: HT 327/4 • NLI: P 212/10
              NLI: P 251/18 • NLI: JP 4852 • NLI: I 6551 Dublin (1799) 7
              BL: 8145 dd 58 • BL: 1509/523 (5) • BL: 8146 ee 23 (3)
                                          Bod: G Pamphlets 1966/10

M6 Memoirs concerning the affairs of Scotland from Queen Anne's accession to the throne to the commencement of the union in May 1707 comprehending an interesting history of that event. By Mr Lockhart. Fourth edition. Dublin: printed for George Folingsby, 1799. xxvi, 402pp.

Date: 'This Day at Twelve o'clock will be published'...5/5d in boards' (DJ 28/2/99 p. 3 col. 4). See hostile notice, associating Jacobitism and Jacobinism, in DJ 28/3/99 p 3 col. 1.
Authorship: George Lockhart (1673-1731) - title-page. Folingsby's advertisement provided additional commentary on Lockhart's indignation at Daniel Defoe's history of the Scottish union, concluding: 'On the first publication of this work which appeared in detached pieces, Mr. Lockhart substituted blanks for the names of the Dramatis Personae. In the second edition he adopted initials and blanks - in the third, party violence having considerably abated, he ventured to add a key for the information of posterity: With this Key the Irish Editor has been enabled to complete the work, by filling up all the blanks; and this the only liberty he deemed it his duty to take with the author.' ESTC notes that the Cork edition is a reissue of the Dublin, but without the 'advertisment to the reader' which preceded the preface.

                                                                    NLI: P 83/3

fourth edition. Cork: J Connor, 1799. xxvi, 402pp.

NLI: I 6551 Cork 1799 • BL: 1480 dd 19

M7 Memoirs of Francis Dobbs; also genuine reports of his speeches in parliament on an union and the second coming of the Messiah, with extracts from his poem on The millennium. Dublin: printed by J Jones, 1800. 68pp.

NLI: P 609/5 • BL: 1609/5573 • Bod: 8 Y 84 (1) Jur.

second edition corrected. Dublin: printed by J Jones, 1800 72pp. (68-72pp ads etc.)

BL: 10857 g 57 (untrimmed)

M8 Memoirs of Lord Rokeby with a prefatory dissertation on beards, also a letter from that venerable nobleman (nearly ninety years old) to the marquis Cornwallis expressing his disapprobation, as an Irish peer, of a legislative union with Great Britain. [Dublin: 1800?] 12pp.

Date: Camillus (probably Sir Richard Musgrave) replies to Rokeby's 'letter ... dated January 22' [1799] which he had seen 'in the public prints' (DJ 19/3/99 p 3 col. 1)

Alston list

M9 Misconceptions of facts and mistatements [sic] of the public accounts by the right hon. John Foster of the Irish House of Commons proved & [sic] corrected according to the official documents and authentic evidence of the Inspector General of Great Britain in a letter to Wm Johnson esq. member of the Irish parliament from the rev. Dr Clarke secretary for the library and chaplain in ordinary to his royal higness the prince of Wales. London: printed for John Hatchard, 1799. 74pp.

Authorship: Thomas Brook Clarke (title-page).
Note: Some copies of the London edition were issued with 'Private tables for this copy' - see pp. [i]-iv in TCD copy.

TCD: 48 g 149 (3) • RLM: PA 1128/9 • CUL: Hib. 5. 799. 20

Dublin: printed for J Milliken, 1800. 60pp.

BLACK 2063, 2205   RIA: HT 341/5 (lacks the prelims paged in little roman nos.) • TCD: Crofton 206/3 (lacks the prelims paged in little roman nos.) • BL: 8145 d 13

second edition. (half-title so describes it)

NLI: P 1509/11

third edition. (half-title so describes it) 56pp. (complete?)

RIA: HT 339/8 • BL: 8145 d 13

fourth edition. (half-title so describes it) 60pp.

RIA: HT 339/7 • NLI: P 112/9

fifth edition. (p. [iii] declares this issue to be a 'fifth edition' and also describes the item as 'being a second appendix to "Union or Separation"'.)

RIA: HP 786/11.

M10 Moggy and Jemmy, or the union feast as was performed at Drury lane Theatre, dedicated with permission to the right honorable Lady Georgiana Cavendish. [ballet for piano forte.] By John Rhodes, the Elder. London: engraved, printed & published by E Riley, [1799.] 10pp.

Authorship: John Rhodes – title-page.
Note: music only.

BL: G 443 g (5)

M11 More thoughts on an union. Dublin: printed by J Moore, 1799. 16pp.

Date: 'Just published' (DJ 10/1/99 p. 3 col.4)
Note: This may be the continuation of T6 below.

BLACK 2126

TCD: V h 23 no. 7 • TCD: 91 p 38 no. 7 (or 6a)
TCD: Lecky A 4 34 no. 1 • TCD: Crofton 184/1
TCD: Crofton 204/1 • RIA: HP 789/ 1 • RIA: HT 321/18
NLI: P 618/9 • BL: 8145 de 8 (5)
Bod: Vet A5 e 5214 • Bod: Vet A5 3 5660

M12 Mr Dobbs's speech in the House of Commons of Ireland on Tuesday the 5th of March 1799 on submitting five propositions for tranquillizing the country. Dublin: printed by J Moore, 1799. 16pp.

RIA: HT 325/1 • RIA: HT 331/9 • NLI: P 609/6 • BL: 1104 c 25 (9)

N

N1 National advantages to be derived from adopting the following plans, viz. I a land-tax in places of tythes, II extension of the woollen and cotton manufactures, III setting the king's commons, IV encreasing the revenue on malt and spirits, V relief of persons confined for debt, VI supplying the poor with coals cheap, VII lending money to the poor at *ten per cent*, VIII cutting a canal from Dublin to Drogheda, IX improving the harbour of Dublin, X supplying the city of Dublin with water at two-thirds of the present expense. By a citizen of Dublin. Dublin: printed by Thomas Morton Bates, 1799. 24pp. + 2 folding charts.

Note: on union, which is more a provocation than a theme, see pp. 22-24.

NLI: P 360/8

N2 Necessity of an incorporate union between Great Britain & [sic] Ireland proved from the situation of both kingdoms, with a sketch of the principles upon which it ought to be formed. Dublin: printed for J Milliken, 1799. 90pp.

Date: advertised DJ 5/3/99 p. 1 col. 2.
Authorship: Milliken advertisement (DJ 5/3/99 p. 1 col. 2) of this item and *Competency* concludes 'These two last pamphlets is [sic] generally attributed to the Pen of a Noble Lord formerly Secretary to L - d Car - le.' A ms note in TCD: Crofton 185 atttributes this item to ' — Nolan Esq of Middle Temple'.
Note: RIA: HT 324/5 title-page bears ms note at bottom 'for Thomas Garde Esq. York Street from Mr O'Shee'.

BLACK 2127   TCD: Crofton 205/4 • RIA: HP 787/ 6 • RIA: HT 318/13
RIA: HT 324/5 • RIA: HT 330/5

second edition. Dublin: printed for J Milliken, 1799. 90pp.

Note: t-p verso of some copies reads 'The following Pamphlet was published in London a few Days previous to his Majesty's message to both Houses of Parliament, recommending a Consolidation of the Strength, Power, and Resources of Great Britain and Ireland.'

RIA: HT 322/2 • RIA: HT 324/7 • RIA: HT 330/4 • NLI: P 128/6
NLI: 618/10 • RLM: 866/5 (with no t-p verso material)
BL: 1103 g 7 (4) (with no t-p verso material)

London: printed for J Wright, 1799. 132pp (plus 1 leaf ads.)

RIA: HT 317/1 • NLI: P 103/1 (incomplete) • BL: 8145 c 20
BL: 111 d 65 • BL: 117 h 31 • CUL: Hib. 5. 798. 3/3

N3 The new doodle doodle doo sung by monsieur Hurdy Gurdy from the Bear-Garden London, at the new circus College-Green *ci devant* the old political theatre. [Dublin:] published at Dowling's, the Apollo Circulating Library, 1800. single sheet.

TCD: S ee 55 (16) • BL: 1325 g 15 (10) • CUL: Hib. 00. 800. 8

N4 New lilla bulero [London? 1800?]. s. sh.

Note: a printed sheet preserved with a letter dated 4/1/[1801] in BL.

BL: Add. Ms. 51592 (11)

N5 A new song. Billy Pitt & the Union. [Dublin, December 1798] single sheet.

NLI: LO 220/1 • BL: 1890 b 8 (7)

N6 No flinching, or a persevering opposition to the measure of an incorporate union strongly recommended. By an eminent barrister. Dublin: printed for J Milliken, 1799. 36p.

Date: Date-line (p. iv of preface) Nov. the 14th 1799; 'this Day is published' (DJ 19/11/

99 p. 2 col 4.)

BLACK 2129   TCD: Crofton 206/10 • RIA: HT 310/3 • RIA: HT 316/8
                    NLI: P 621/5 (untrimmed) • CUL: Hib. 5. 799. 71

N7 No union! being an appeal to Irishmen. By Matthew Weld. Dublin: printed
by H Fitzpatrick, 1798. 32pp. [pp. 30-32 blank]

Date: copies of the 2nd and 3rd editions bear ms datings which probably refer to first
publication of the title, e.g. RIA: HP 766/3 title-page ms note reads 'early in Decr.' and
RIA: 308/9 blue wrapper reads in ms 'published early in Decr 1798'.
Authorship: Matthew Weld - title-page.
Note: this text, its title modified with varying numbers of exclamation marks, was issued
by at least three different Dublin booksellers (Fitzpatrick, Smith, and M'Donald), and
under two distinct Cork imprints.

                                             BL: 1570/5786

second edition. By Matthew Weld. Dublin: printed by H Fitzpatrick, 1798. 32pp.
[pp. 30-32 blank]

                          RIA: HP 766/3 • RIA: HT 308/5
                    NLI: I 6551 Dublin 1798 • BL: 8145 dd 74

third edition. By Matthew Weld. Dublin: printed by H Fitzpatrick, 1798. 32pp.
[pp. 30-32 blank]

              RIA: HT 308/8 • RLM: PA 866/3 (lacks final blank leaf)

fourth edition, with additions and corrections. Dublin: printed by H Fitzpatrick,
1798. 32pp. [p. 32 blank]

        TCD: V h 21 no. 4 • RIA: HT 308/7 • NLI: P 2/4 • NLI: P 251/5
                                             BL: 1509/523 (1)

fourth edition. Cork: printed by J Haly, 1798. 24pp.

                          NLI: JP 344 • BL: 1608/3705

fourth edition. Cork: printed by J Haly, M Harris, and J Connor, 1798. 24pp.

                                             RLM: PA 35/14

fifth edition, with additions and corrections. Dublin: printed by H Fitzpatrick,
1798. 32pp.

                    TCD: Lecky A 4 32 no. 3 • RIA: HT 307/14

N8 No union!! being an appeal to Irishmen.
third edition. Dublin: printed by R M'Donald, 1798. 22pp.

Authorship: Matthew Weld - title-page.

RIA: HT 307/4 • RIA: HT 306/3

N9 No union, being an appeal to Irishmen. By Matthew Weld.
second edition. Dublin: [no pr.], 1798. 20pp.

Authorship: Matthew Weld - title-page.

RIA: HT 307/8

second edition. Dublin: printed by Brett Smith, 1798. 20pp.

TCD: Crofton 182/4

N10 No union! But unite and fall. By Paddy Whack of Dyott-street London in a loving letter to his dear mother Sheelah of Dame-Street Dublin. [London:] Dublin printed: London reprinted and sold by W J and J Richardson [et al], 1799. 40pp.

Authorship: John Fitzgibbon, earl of Clare; so assigned in a ms. note on BL: 112 a 41.

BL: 112 a 42

second edition. [London:] Dublin printed: London reprinted and sold by W J and J Richardson [et al], 1799. 40pp.

BL: 112 a 41

N11 No union for our dear native land [Song, 'May God in whose hands...'] Dublin: published by Hime, [1800.] 4pp.

Note: in verse (5 stanzas).

BL: H 1653 j (66)

O

O1 Observations on Arguments for and against an union between Great Britain and Ireland. Dublin: printed by J Stockdale, 1799. 16pp.

Authorship: Signs off, (p. 15) F L

BLACK 2131   TCD: V h 21 no. 12 • RIA: HT 331/13 • NLI: P 212/7
NLI: P 251/9 • NLI: 618/12

O2 Observations on the commercial principles of the projected union, or a free examination of the sixth resolution being the only one that touches upon commerce and carrying a direct commission to appropriate Ireland and for ever as a consuming colony to the British manufacturer. London: printed for R Pitkeathley, 1800. 68pp.

Authorship: assigned to Harding Giffard in ms note on the fly-leaf of TCD: Crofton 190 (containing an incomplete copy of this item.)

TCD: 91 q 17 (6) • Goldsmiths Coll. 17853

O3 Observations on Dr Duigenan's Fair representation of the present political state of Ireland, particularly with respect to his strictures on a pamphlet entitled The case of Ireland reconsidered. By Patrick Lattin. London: [printed by T Burton and] sold by J Debrett, 1800. 128pp.

Authorship: Patrick Lattin (title-page).

TCD: 91 q 7 (11) • RLM: PA 1127/3

O4 Observations on Mr Bousfield's Letter etc. Cork: printed at the Cork Advertiser Office, 1799. 18pp.

Date: Cork, Feb. 16, 1799 (p. 18)
Authorship: signed (p. 18) A Freeman.

UCC: Stopford Pamphlets 277

O5 Observations on a pamphlet entitled The speech of the right hon. John Beresford on his moving the sixth article of the union. By a friend of the speaker's. Dublin: printed for J Moore, 1800. 34pp.

RIA: HP 797/9 • RIA: HT 334/20 • RIA: HT 335/20
                              NLI: P 2501/4 • BL: 1508/1560

O6 Observations on a pamphlet supposed to be written by an Englishman, entitled Arguments for and against an union. By a student of Trinity College. Dublin: printed by J Milliken, 1799. 32pp.

Date: 'Just published' (DJ 8/1/99 p. 2 col. 4).
Note: with errata at bottom of p. 32.

TCD: V h 25 no. 5 • TCD: Lecky A 4 33 no. 12
               TCD: Crofton 203/8 • RIA: HP 767/ 15 • RIA: HT 321/12
               RIA: HT 327/6 • BL: 8145 de 9 (8) • BL: 8146 f 34 (4)

O7 Observations on some passages in the publications of a citizen of Dublin, lately disenfranchised in a letter from Hypodidascalus to the right honorable B. Lord Yelverton. Dublin: printed in the year 1800. 34pp.

RIA: HP 805/2 • BL: 1609/5006

O8 Observations on that part of the speaker's speech which relates to trade. Dublin: printed by T Burnside, 1799. 44pp. + folding tables.

Date: 'this Day is published' (DJ 13/8/99 p. 1 col. 2.)
Authorship: R Longfield, viscount Longueville; see presentation copy (of a Cork ed.) from the author to Wm. Pitt in Goldsmiths Collection; attributed by BL to John Beresford; RLM copy assigned to Beresford in a contemporary title-page annotation.
Note: The Dublin (Burnside) edition certainly exists in different states; cf the catch-words

on p. 43 in BL: 8135 ccc 1 (10) and 8145 d 30.

BLACK 2133   RIA: HP 788/ 2 • RIA: HT 315/10 • RIA: HT 315/13
            NLI: P 155/3 • NLI: P 618/13 • NLI: JP 334 • RLM: 871/4
        BL: 8135 ccc 1 (10) • BL: 8145 d 30 • BL: 6837 d 8 (11) (mutilated)
        RIA: HT 334/17 (lacks title-page etc.) • CUL: Hib. 5. 799. 80

Belfast: printed by E Black [1799] 38pp + folding tables etc.

BL: 1578/3422

Cork: printed by George Cherry (for the proprietors) at the Advertising-office,
1799. 52pp + folding tables.

NLI: I 6551 Cork 1799 • BL: 1560/1256 (2)

O9 Observations on the speech of the right honorable John Foster, speaker of the
House of Commons of Ireland, delivered there April 11 1799. By a gentleman at
the bar. London: printed for the author and sold by J Downes [et al.], 1799.
64pp.

Date: CUL copy has 'July 1st' inserted in ms in imprint.
Authorship: Black accepts Joseph Downes (title-page, imprint) as author.

BLACK 2076   RIA: HT 321/15 • BL: 117 h 25 • BL: 111 d 66
CUL: Hib. 5. 799. 79

O10 Observations on the union, Orange associations and other subjects of
domestic policy, with reflections on the late events on the continent. By George
Moore. Dublin: printed by H Fitzpatrick, 1799. 80pp.

Authorship: George Moore (title page) barrister, of Lincoln's Inn.

BLACK 2247   TCD: Crofton 206/9 • RIA: HP 780/4 • RIA: HT 317/17
            NLI: I 6551 (Dublin) 1 • BL: 1103 g 8 (4)

second edition with an appendix. Dublin: printed by H Fitzpatrick, 1800. 102pp.

RIA: HT 341/4

[London:] Dublin printed; London: re-printed for J Debrett, 1800. 80pp.

RIA: HT 337/1 • BL: 117 h 44 (1) • CUL: Hib. 5. 800. 53

A new edition to which is added an appendix, suggested by the late debates in the
Irish parliament and the resolutions of certain public bodies of the city of Dublin.
[London:] Dublin printed; London re-printed for J Debrett, 1800. 104pp.

NLI: P 103/2

O11 An ode in deprecation of an odious measure, addressed to a great assembly.

By Tim. Pindar, an Irish relation of the Theban bard. Dublin: published by V
Dowling at the Apollo Circulating Library, 1799. 14pp.

Note: in verse.

TCD: V h 25 no. 1 • RIA: HT 316/ 3 • BL: 1609/5118

O12 The olio or anything-arian miscellany. Dublin: printed for the editor and
published by Dowling, [1800]. 6 issues = 48pp.

Note: this is part of the Pimlico material.

TCD: S ee 55 (8) • BL: P. P. 3727 (3) • Bod: Vet A5 d 629/2
CUL: Hib. 4. 799. 1/2

O13 On the union. Air 'The duchess'. [with] Granu Wale. [Dublin:] published
at Dowling's, the Apollo Circulating Library, [1800.]

TCD: S ee 55 (15) • BL: 1325 g 15 (7) • CUL: Hib. oo. 800. 7

O14 On Wednesday 15th January, Royal Circus College-Green, by particular
desire; the manager respectfully informs his friends and the public that the
celebrated piece, called The union, or Ierne divided! with many alterations and
additions which brought such overflowing houses last year and which went off
with so much satisfaction to the public is again in rehearsal. [Dublin, n. p. 1800]
single sheet.

CUL: Hib. oo. 800. 10

O15 Orange, a political rhapsody. Canto I. Dublin [n. p.] 1797. 16pp.

TCD: 91 q 2 (8)

O16 Orange, a political rhapsody. Canto II. Dublin [n. p.] 1798. 20pp.

TCD: 91 q 2 (9) • RLM: PA 39/6

O17 Orange, a political rhapsody. Canto III. Dublin: printed for John Milliken,
1798. 24pp.

RLM: PA 39/7

O18 Orange, a political rhapsody in three cantos.

Note to O 15-18 : there is only passing reference to union, as this portmanteau text was
written and first published before the debates under examination commenced. Its
maintenance in print reflects the many allusions to writers taking part in the exchange of
union pamphlets.

seventh edition. Dublin: printed for John Milliken, 1798. 76pp.

TCD: Lecky A 3 17 no. 8

ninth edition. Dublin: printed for John Milliken, 1798. 22, 24, 24pp.

TCD: Crofton 142/4

O19 Orange vindicated in a reply to Theobald M'Kenna esq., with observations on the new and further claims of the Catholics as affecting the constitution and the protestant establishment. A new edition revised and enlarged with notes by the author. Dublin: printed by William M'Kenzie, 1799. 64pp.

Authorship: signed (p. 43) An Orangeman.
Date: date-lines (p. 43) Dublin January 14, 1799, (p. 50) Dublin January 22 1799.

RIA: HT 310/5 • RIA: HT 332/5 • RLM: PA 21/10
UCC: Stopford Pamphlets 279 • BL: 8146 cc 30

fourth edition, revised and enlarged with notes by the author. Dublin: printed by William M'Kenzie, 1799. 64pp.

Date: 'This day is published' (DJ 16/5/99 p. 3 col 1.)

RIA: HP 780/ 9

a new edition. Sixth edition revised and enlarged with notes by the author. Dublin: printed by William M'Kenzie, 1799. 60pp.

BL: 1609/4037

P

P1 Paddy the pointer to the staunch dogs of Ireland. Air 'Bow, wow, wow'. [with] Unanimity against union, a British ballad somewhat altered for the use of Irishmen. Air 'Success to the duchess'. [Dublin:] published at Dowling's, the Apollo Circulating Library, [1800]. single sheet.

TCD: S ee 55 (14) • CUL: Hib. oo. 800. 6

P2 Parliamentary register; or, history of the proceedings and debates of the House of Commons of Ireland, which met at Dublin on Wednesday the 18th [sic] of January 1800. Part the first. Dublin: printed for John Milliken, 1800. 144pp.

Note: the date of debate should read 15th of January.

TCD: Lecky A 3 48 (13) • CUL: Hib. 5. 800. 39

P3 Parliamentary register, or history of the proceedings and debates of the House of Commons of Ireland, which met at Dublin on Wednesday the 15th of January 1800; part the first on Sir Laurence Parsons amendment on the address to his majesty; part the second on the king's message recommending a legislative union; part the third the house in a committee on the further considerationa of his majesty's message. Dublin: printed for J Milliken, 1800. 144pp.

TCD: Crofton 209/11 • RIA: HT 340/5

P4 The patriot's return, a lyric ode dedicated to the thrice honorable Henry Grattan esq on his welcome return to the senate of his distracted country at the most critical moment of her existence. Dublin: printed by Vincent Dowling, 1800. 10pp.

Note: in verse; see p. 8 re union.

TCD: S ee 55 (9) • RIA: HT 336/10 • CUL: Hib. 4. 799.1/3

P5 The peace offering . Songs on the signing of preliminaries and ratification of peace, October 1st and 10th 1801 By J Brisset, museum Birmingham. Also the Irish union and several miscellaneous songs. Birmingham: printed by Grofton & Reddell for the author, 1801. 36pp.

Authorship: James Bisset, (ca. 1762-1832).
Note: see pp. 18-19 re. union.

BL: 11601 dd 27 (1)

P6 The philleleu, or an arithmetical calculation of the losses which the trade & [sic] property of Ireland and of the empire in general must sustain by an union. Dublin: printed by Joseph Mehain, 1799. 8pp.

BLACK 2137   TCD: V h 24 no. 7 • RIA: HT 316/5 • KID: 45/10

P7 Pitt's union. Dublin: printed by J Stockdale, 1799. 24pp.

Authorship: W. J. MacNeven (1763-1841) for attribution to 'MacNeven' see TCD: V h 25 no. 3 and Crofton 185/4

BLACK 2141   TCD: V h 25 no. 3 • TCD: Crofton 185/4 • RIA: HT 324/6
                    RIA: HT 331/16 • NLI: P 623/5 • BL: 8145 c

P8 Plain truths and correct statements of facts in reply to Mr Grattan's answer to the lord chancellor's speech. By a looker-on. Dublin: printed by W Corbet, 1800. 56pp.

Date: date-line (p. 53) 28th April, 1800.
Authorship: ms note on fly-leaf of TCD: Crofton 190 assigns this item to 'William Corbett Bookseller' [i.e. issuer of the item].
Note: some copies have errata slip pasted to p. [56].

TCD: Crofton 190 (3) • TCD: Crofton 210 (2) • RIA: HT 336/25
                    RIA: HT 339/5 • NLI: P 622/14 • BL: 8145 dd 55

second edition. Dublin: printed by W Corbet, 1800. 58pp.

RIA: HP 805/1

P9 The political, commercial and civil state of Ireland, being an apprendix to "Union or Separation". By the rev. Dr Clarke. London: printed for J Hatchard [et al], 1799. 82pp.

Date: 'This Day Published' by Milliken (DJ 8/6/99 p. 3 col 4.).
Authorship: Thomas Brook Clarke (title-page).

BLACK 2064   TCD: 48 g 149 (2) • RLM: PA 1128/8 • BL: 505 (4)
                                          BL: 111 d 52 • BL: 117 h 38

Dublin: printed for J Milliken, 1799. 70pp.

                    TCD: Crofton 206/2 • RIA: HP 786/ 3 • RIA: HT 322/12
            NLI: P 609/2 (untrimmed) • RLM: PA 869/3 • BL: 8145 dd 10
                              BL: 1609/5064 • Bod: 226 i 168/17

P10 Positive John: or nothing can cure him, a new lyric ballad on the union. [Dublin:] sold at Dowling's, [1800.] single sheet.

                    TCD: S ee 55 (11) • BL: 1325 g 15 (11)
                    Bod: Vet A5 a 14 • CUL: Hib. oo. 800. 3

P11 Practical observations on the proposed treaty of union of the legislatures of Great Britain and Ireland shewing in some particulars how that treaty may be rendered acceptable to the people of Ireland and beneficial to the British empire in general, By John Gray. London: printed for T Beckett [et al], 1800. 104pp. (printed by G Woodfall, London)

Authorship: John Gray - title-page.

BLACK 2233   RIA: HT 339/10 (bottom of t-p damaged) • BL: 8145 cc 35

P12 The present state of Ireland and the only means of preserving her to the empire considered in a letter to the marquis Cornwallis. By James Geraghty. London: printed for J Stockdale, 1799. 50pp.

Authorship: James Geraghty (title-page).

BLACK 2091   TCD: V h 23 no. 5 • TCD: Crofton 205/7 • RIA: HP 787/ 9
                    RIA: HT 318/14 • RIA: HT 321/4 • RIA: HT 324/12
                    NLI: P 112/4 • BL: 8146 f 34 (12) • BL: 117 h 5

[same imprint, but with author's name spelled Gerahty] 84pp.

                    NLI: P 112/4 (with leaf of ads. between t-p and text)
                    BL: 117 h 5 (without leaf of ads.)

P13 The principles of the Orange association stated and vindicated in a discourse before the members of the Orange societies in Lisburn district, July 12 1799; and published at their particular request by the Rev S Cupples. Belfast: printed by Doherty & Simms, [1799.] 19pp surviving.

Authorship: S Cupples - title-page.
Note: Includes (pp. 18-19) the declaration of the Grand Lodge of Ireland, 5 January 1799,

advising the organisation to adopt a policy of silence on the issue of union, irrespective of the views expressed by individual members in their several political roles.

Linenhall Library, Belfast - BPB 1799.5 (photocopy)
CUL: Hib. 7. 799. 7

P14 A private acknowledgement for public services in an epistle to the glorious one hundred and eleven. By a friend to Ireland. Dublin: for Bernard Dornin, 1799. 66pp.

Date: 'This Day was published' (DJ 1/6/99 p. 2 col. 4)

Authorship: Signs off (p. 65) C K.

RIA: HT 314/2 • NLI: I 6551 Dublin 1799
Free Library of Pennsylvania: Dublin 1799 Private (lacks pp. 57-64)

P15 Pro and con: being an impartial abstract of the principal publications on the subject of a legislative union between Great Britain and Ireland, in which the arguments for and against that measure, by the following writers, are fairly contrasted, viz. earl of Clare, lord Auckland, lord Minto, rt hon. Mr Addington, rt hon. Mr Pitt, rt hon. Mr Dundas, rt hon. Mr Douglas, Dean Tucker, Mr Wm Smith, Dr Clarke, Mr Peele, Dr M'Kenna, earl of Farnham, rt hon. Mr Foster, Sir J W Jervis bt, Mr Spencer, Mr Bousfield, Mr Edgeworth, Mr Rudd, Mr Goold, Mr Taaffe, Mr Weld, Mr Sheehy, Dr Drennan; also Arguments for and against etc, Cease your funning, Impartial view of the causes leading to etc, Tit for tat, and many other anonymous writers on this subject. By a searcher after truth. Dublin: printed and sold by Marchbank, 1800. 88pp.

Authorship: ms note in TCD: Crofton 190 assigns this item to Revd Doctor Beaufort', [i.e. Daniel Beaufort]
Note: Some effort appears to have been made to arrange for a London edition, see ms. inscription 'This copy is sent to Mr Wright by the Author; that he may publish it if he thinks proper.' on CUL: Hib. 5. 800. 70.

BLACK 2257   TCD: - Crofton 190 (1) • TCD: Crofton 210/1
RIA: HP 805/5 • NLI: P 401/11 • NLI: P 623/16 • BL: 1568/8166
CUL: Hib. 5. 800. 70 • CUL: Hib. 5. 800. 71

P16 The probability, causes and consequences of an union between Great Britain and Ireland discussed, with strictures on an anonymous pamphlet in favour of the measure supposed to be written by a gentleman high in office. By the rev. Dennis Taaffe. Dublin: printed by J Hill, 1798. 48pp.

Date: RIA: HP 766/8 t-p ms note reads 'pub. 10 Dec 1798'.

BLACK 2033   TCD: V h 21 no. 8 • TCD: 91 p 38 no. 9
TCD: Lecky A 4 32 no. 8 • RIA: HP 766/8
RIA: HT 307/3 • NLI: P 221/7 • NLI: P 251/6
BL: 1509/523 (4) • BL: 8145 bbb 56 (2)

P17 The probable consequences of a union impartially considered. By a barrister. Dublin: printed for J Milliken, 1799. 18pp.

Date: 'Just published' (DJ 8/1/99 p. 2 col. 4).
Authorship: attributed to William Johnson, by Black.

BLACK 2104, 2143   TCD: V h 23 no. 15 • TCD: Lecky A 4 33 no. 11
TCD: Crofton 203 (7) • RIA: HP 767/13
RIA: HT 331/11 • NLI: P 2/14 • NLI: I 6551 Dublin 1799
BL: 117 h 39 • BL: 111 d 68

P18 Proceedings and debates of the parliament of Pimlico in the last session of the eighteenth century. Triplio [i.e. Dublin:] pubished by the executors of Judith Freel, late publisher to his Dalkeian majesty and sold at No. 5 College Green, 1799-1800. [nos. 1-28, each 4pp.]

Authorship/editorship: Attributed, *tout court*, to Vincent Dowling (a bookseller) by Halkett and Laing.

TCD: S ee 55 (7) • Bod: Vet A5 d 629/1 • BL: 1325 g 15 (5)
BL: P. P. 3727 (2) • CUL: Hib. 4. 799. 1/6 (with 2pp. ms key)

P19 Proceedings at a meeting of the bankers and merchants of Dublin convened by the right hon. the lord mayor on Tuesday December 18th 1798 for the purpose of considering the subject of an union. Dublin: printed by V Dowling, 1798. 16pp.

Date: Advertised DJ 20/12/98 for publication on 22/12/98.

BLACK 2025   TCD: V h 22 no. 3 • RIA: HT 307/9 (this copy has extra 4pp of ads.) • NLI: P 618/15 • BL: 8145 de 8 (9)

P20 Proceedings at a meeting of the gentlemen, clergy, and freeholders of the county of Dublin on Friday January the 4th 1799 to take into consideration the measure of a legislative union between this country and Great Britain; Alexander Kirkpatrick esq. high sheriff in the chair; in which is a correct report of Mr Spencer's speech. Dublin: printed for William Jones, 1799. 28pp.

BLACK 2144   TCD: V h 23 no. 10 • TCD: Lecky A 4 33 no. 19
(with half-title) • RIA: HP 767/ 19 • RIA: HT 318/5
RIA: HT 328/2 • NLI: P 618/16 • NLI: I 6551 Dublin (1799) 10
BL: 8145 de 8 (10) • BL: 8146 f 34 (9) (with half-title)

P21 Proceedings of the parliament of Ireland, 1799. Dublin: printed for W M'Kenzie, 1799. 48pp. (incomplete)

Note: The RIA copy retains a blue paper upper cover, from which one can deduce that this was the first in a projected series of weekly publications.

RIA: HT 321/8

P22 Projects for re-establishing the internal peace and tranquillity of Ireland. By

Whitley Stokes. Dublin: printed for James Moore, 1799. 52pp.

Date: an advertisement for an untraced title, similar to this, appeared in DJ 7/2/99 and 12/2/99: see list of such items at the conclusion of the alphabetical list.
Authorship: Whitley Stokes (title-page).
Note: Half-title (see NLI and BL copies) reads *Peace of Ireland.*

BLACK 2168   TCD: V h 24 no. 4 • RIA: HT 315/8 • RIA: HT 316/4
                    NLI: I 655 Dublin (1799) 8 • BL: 8146 f 34 (7)

P23 Proofs rise on proofs, that the union is totally incompatible with the rights of the ancient, self-legislative and independent kingdom of Ireland, however embellished and flattering its introduction may appear. Dublin: printed and sold by Marchbank [et al.], 1799. 40pp.

Date: 'This Day was Published' (DJ 17/1/99 p. 4 col. 4).
BLACK 2145   TCD: V h 24 no. 1 • TCD: Lecky A 4 34 no. 8
             TCD: Crofton 204 (8) • RIA: HT 310/12 • RIA: HT 311/18
                              RIA: HT 331/20 • BL: 8145 dd 45

P24 A proposal for uniting the kingdoms of Great Britain and Ireland. London: printed for J Hatchard, 1800. 36pp.

Authorship: Ms note on half-title of RIA: 805/7 reads 'This pamphlet is attributed to the late earl of Hilsborough.' Black suggests 'Downshire, Arthur Hill, 2nd marquess?' BL suggests 'Wills Hill, marquis of Downsire'. Half-title states 'printed by J Bateson, Denmark street, Soho'. Its verso reads 'It is only necessary to inform the reader, that this pamphlet was originally printed for A Millar, in the Strand, in 1751; and is now carefully reprinted from that Edition without note or alteration. January 1800.' For the 1751 publication, see BL: 110 e 40.

BLACK 2212   RIA: 805/ 7 • RIA: HT 341/2 (without half-title)
                                           NLI: P 618/17

P25 The proposition, A new song on the union. Air 'Paddy Whack' [Dublin:] published at Dowling's, the Apollo Circulating Library, [1799.] single sheet.

                    TCD: S ee 55 (13) • CUL: Hib. oo.8oo. 5

P26 The prospect before us, or Great Britain and Ireland one and indivisible, being free thoughts on the first of January 1801. Dublin: printed for J Milliken, 1801. 24pp.

                    RIA: HT 344/2 (large paper copy) • RIA: HT 344/7
                              NLI: P 618/18 • RLM: PA 1044/10

P27 A protest from one of the people of Ireland against an union with Great Britain. Dublin: printed by George Folingsby, 1800. 14pp.

Date and authorship: William Drennan. Signs off, p. 14, William Drennan January 6.

                    RIA: HP 805/9 • NLI: P 125/1 • NLI: P 609/11

P28 Protestant ascendancy and Catholic emancipation reconciled by a legislative union, with a view of the transactions in 1782 relative to the independence of the Irish parliament, and the present political state of Ireland as dependant on the crown and connected with the parliament of Great Britain; with an appendix. London: printed [by S Gosnell] for J Wright, 1800. 142pp.

Authorship: William Ogilvie - so attributed in Bradshaw and in RIA copy. Ms note in TCD: Crofton 190 (5) assigns this item to 'Ogilvie who married the Duchess of Leinster'. Note: issued with half-title and three final pages of advertisements. See also below.

BLACK 2258   RIA: HP 797/1 • BL: 117 h 43 • Bod: Vet A5 e 6140
CUL: Hib. 7. 800. 27 • CUL: Hib. 800. 65 • CUL: Hib. 5. 798. 3/2

Dublin: printed for J Milliken, 1800. 120pp.

Note: issued with half-title and no advertisments. The RIA copy is in original state, with owner/customer's name, The revd Mr Little, Killalla, on wrapper.

TCD: Crofton 190 (5) • RIA: HT 341/3 • NLI: P 618/19 (t-p damaged)

R

R1 Reasons against a union in which "Arguments for and against a union", supposed to have come from a person in high station, are particularly considered. By an Irishman. Dublin: printed for G Folingsby, 1798. 32pp.
Date: title-page ms note in RIA: HP 766/13 reads 'published on 16 Decr 1798'.

Authorship: attributed to 'John Kelly esq Ship-Street' in TCD: Crofton 182 fly-leaf list.
BLACK 2026   TCD: V h 21 no. 15 • TCD: Lecky A 4 32 no. 11
TCD: Crofton 182/8 (lacks t-p) • RIA: HP 766/ 14
NLI: P 251/12 • BL: 1509/523 (9) • Bod: G Pamphlets 2758/5

second edition. Dublin: printed for G Folingsby, 1798. 32pp.

TCD: Crofton 202/7 • RIA: HT 307/1
NLI: P 221/10 • BL: 8145 de 9 (6)

R2 Reasons for adopting an union between Ireland and Great Britain. By the author of the Letter to Jos. Spencer esq. Dublin: printed for J Milliken, 1799. 62pp.

Date; - - 'This Day is Published' (DJ 19/1/99 p. 3 col. 4).
Authorship: William Johnson (title-page of second edition); A note on the fly-leaf of TCD: V h 25 attributes this item to 'William Johnson, Barrister'.

BLACK 2105, 2237   TCD: V h 25 no. 4 • RIA: HP 789/8 • RIA: HT 305/6
(2nd item) • RIA: HT 333/7 (with 4pp. list of pamphlets)
NLI: P 112/2 • NLI: P 156/2 • NLI: 619/1
BL: 117 h 30 • Bod: Vet A5 e 5670

second edition corrected. By William Johnson. Dublin: printed for J Milliken,

1799. 62pp.

Date: 'this day published' (DJ 16/2/99 p. 3 col. 4).

> RIA: HT 315/4 • RIA: HT 316/12 • RIA: HT 317/10
> RIA: HT 325/5 • NLI: P 612/9 • RLM: PA 25/7

fourth edition. By William Johnson. Dublin: printed for J Milliken, 1799. 60pp.

> NLI: P 612/8

fourth edition. By William Johnson. Dublin: printed for J Milliken, 1799. 62pp.
Note: with catch-word on p. 60.

> RIA: HT 317/4 • RIA: HP 789/ 7 • BL: 1103 g 10 (2)

fifth edition. By William Johnson. Dublin: printed for J Milliken, 1799. 62pp.

> TCD: Lecky A 4 34 no. 10 • RIA: HT 321/5
> BL: 111 d 61 • Bod: Vet A5 5215

sixth edition. With a preface now first published. By William Johnson Dublin: printed for J Milliken, 1800. 62pp.

Date: date-line (p. xxvi) Jan 13 1800; (preface pp. i-xxvi).

> TCD: Crofton 184/9 • TCD: Crofton 204/10
> RIA: HT 334/19 (ms note on the t-p verse reads
> 'For the lord bishop of Meath with the
> greatest respect from the Author.')
> RIA: HT 334/11 (on lighter paper than 334/19 which is clearly a
> presentation state.) • RIA: HT 337/7 (heavy paper)
> BL: 1609/2127 • CUL: Hib. 7. 800. 16

By the author of the Letter to Jos. Spencer. London: printed by J Plymsell at the Anti-Jacobin Press, [1799.] 62pp.

> CUL: Hib. 5. 799. 50

second edition. By the author of the letter to Jos Spencer esq. London: printed by J Plymsell at the Anti-Jacobin Press, [1799]. 62pp.

> RIA: HT 333/unnumbered

fifth edition. London: printed for J Wright, 1799. 62pp.

> RLM: PA 1128/5 • CUL: Hib 5. 799. 51 • CUL: Hib. 5. 798. 3/5

R3 Refutation of Dr Duigenan's appendix; or an attempt to ascertain the extent, population and wealth of Ireland, and the relative numbers as well as property of the protestant and Roman Catholic inhabitants. London: printed for J Stockdale,

1800. 78pp.

Note: p. 45 relates this work to *Arguments for and against an union.*

BLACK 2260 RIA: HT 337/10 • BL: 3942 f 2 • CUL: Hib. 5. 800. 24

R4 Remarks on a pamphlet entitled 'Arguments for and against an union. By a farmer. Dublin: printed for the book-sellers, 1799. 48pp.

BLACK 2146 RIA: HT 336/19

R5 Remarks on the terms of the union. By Arthur Browne. Dublin [n. pub], 1800. 24pp.

Authorship: Arthur Brown (1756?-1805) - title-page.

BLACK 2199 RIA: HT 335/17 • NLI: P 607/13

R6 A reply to the gentleman who has published a pamphlet entitled "Arguments for and against an union" in which Mr M'Kenna's Memoire is taken into consideration. By Isaac Burke Bethel. Dublin: printed by W Gilbert, 1799. 32pp.

Date: 'To-morrow will be published (DJ 1/1/99 p. 2 col. 4); 'This Day is published' (DJ 3/1/99 p. 3 col. 4).
Authorship: Isaac Burke Bethel (title-page).

BLACK 2052 TCD: V h 23 no. 3 • RIA: HT 327/2 • BL: 8145 cc 6

R7 A reply to the Memoire of Theobald McKenna esq. on some questions touching the projected union of Great-Britain and Ireland. By Molyneux [pseud?]. Dublin: printed by H Fitzpatrick, 1799. 36pp.

Authorship: BL attributes this to Sir Capel Molyneux; Black attributes it to William Philip Molyneux (later 1st baron Sefton). But a note on the vol fly-leaf of TCD: V h 23 attributes this to 'Thomas Grady, chairman of Limerick County'.)

BLACK 2125 TCD: V h 23 no. 1 • TCD: Lecky A 4 33 no. 18
RIA: 327/5 • BL: 8145 de 12 (2)

R8 Reply to a ministerial pamphlet entitled "Considerations upon the state of public affairs in the year 1799: " Ireland". By a philanthropist. Dublin: printed and sold by the booksellers, 1799. 48pp.

Date: signs off, p. 46, June 30th 1799.

RIA: HT 316/14 • RIA: HT 327/3 • BL: 8145 dd 63
CUL: Hib. 5 798. 68 (11)

[same imprint] 24pp.

Date: signs off p. 24, June 30th 1799.

RLM: PA 23/10

R9 A reply to a pamphlet entitled Arguments for and against an union. By Richard Jebb. Dublin: printed for William Jones, 1798. 68pp.

Date: 'Bushe, Barrington and Mr Jebb come forth in print to-morrow.' Alexander Knox to Castlereagh, letter dated Friday [following 15/12/98], quoted in Castlereagh *Correspondence* vol 2 p. 45.
Authorship: Richard Jebb (1766-1834) - title-page.

BLACK 2010, 2102, 2103   TCD: Crofton 203/2 • RIA: HP 767/ 2
                        RIA: HT 332/7 • NLI: P 251/13 • NLI: 612/4
                        BL: 1570/1614 • Bod: G Pamphlets 2758/7

second edition. Dublin: printed for William Jones, 1798. 68pp

                TCD: V h 22 no. 5 • RIA: HP 767/ 3 • RIA: HT 303/15
                        RIA: HT 307/2 • NLI: P 612/5 • NLI: JP 3354
                                BL: 8145 d 57 • BL: 117 h 16 (1)
                        Bod: G Pamphlets 1965/3 (lacks pp. 65-end.)

third edition. Dublin: printed for William Jones, 1799. 50pp.

                TCD: Lecky A 4 33 no. 2 • RIA: HP 767/ 4 • NLI: P 612/6
                                        NLI: I 6551 Dublin (1799) 9

[London:] Dublin printed; London reprinted for J Debrett, 1799. 68pp.

                TCD: Crofton 203/2 • BL: 111 d 40 (1) • BL: 117 h 16 (1)

R10 A reply to the speech delivered in the Irish House of Commons Wednesday Jan 15 1800, by Mr Grattan on the subject of a legislative union. By an absentee. Bath: printed by S Hazard, sold by Hatchard, London, 1800. 18pp.

                                                NLI: P 621/1

R11 A reply to the speech of the speaker [i.e. John Foster] as stated to have been delivered on the 17th of February 1800. Dublin: printed by John Rea, 1800. 66pp.

Authorship: William Cusack Smith, so attributed in ms note on t-p of the Sheffield copy in Goldsmiths Coll.; RLM copy has title-page inscription 'by William Johnson'; a note on the fly-leaf of TCD: Crofton 189 reads 'The Reply to the Speaker's Speech was wrote by Mr Beresford'.

BLACK 2261   RIA: HP 806/7 • NLI: P 156/7 • NLI: P 619/2
                        RLM: PA 871/6 • BL: 1609/5092

third edition. Dublin: printed by John Rea, 1800. 66pp.

                TCD: Crofton 189 (11) • RIA: HT 336/26 • NLI: P 226/5

fourth edition. Dublin: printed by John Rea, 1800. 66pp.

RLM: PA 753/7 • RLM: 342/2 • BL: 8145 aaa 38 • CUL: Hib: 5. 800. 60

fifth edition. Dublin: printed by John Rea, 1800. 66pp.

TCD: Crofton 206/5

R12 Report of the debate in the House of Commons of Ireland on Friday the 14th of February 1800 on the subject of a legislative union with Great Britain, containing the speeches of the right hon. the speaker, messrs Ponsonby, lord Castlereagh, Egan, Smith, Saurin, Johnson, O'Donnell, Burrowes, the right hon. the chancellor of the exchequer, and the reply of Henry Grattan esq; also the petitions from the county of Carlow, county of the town of Carrickfergus, merchants, traders etc of the town of Newry, county of Down, King's county, county of Leitrim, county of West-meath, county of Clare, borough of Downpatrick, freeholders and inhabitants of Portarlington, and counties of Louth and Cork. Dublin: printed by J Milliken and J Rice, 1800. 84pp.

BLACK 2263   TCD: Crofton 209/13
                                    NLI: P 619/8 • CUL: Hib. 5. 800. 41

Dublin: printed by J Stockdale, 1800. 84pp.

CUL: Hib. 5. 798. 68 (21)

R13 A report of the debate in the House of Commons of Ireland on Tuesday and Wednesday the 22nd and 23d of January 1799 on the subject of an union. [The drop title is The parliamentary register.] Dublin: printed for James Moore, 1799. 92pp.

BLACK 2149   TCD: 91 p 38 no. 10 • RIA: HT 313/9 • RIA: HT 322/1
                            (in original blue paper covers.) • RIA: HT 330/3
            NLI: P 619/4 • Bod: G Pamphlets 1967/1 • CUL: Hib. 5. 799. 41

R14 A report of the debate in the House of Commons of Ireland on Tuesday and Wednesday the 22nd and 23rd of January 1799 on the subject of an union. Dublin: printed for James Moore, 1799. 166pp.

TCD: V h 25 no. 9
RIA: HP 786/ 6 (with second title-page between pp. [92] and 93.
RLM: PA 872/1 (with second title-page)
BL: 287 g 14 (2) • Bod: G Pamphlets 1967/1

R15 A report of the debate in the House of Commons of Ireland on the 24th, 25th, 26th and 28th of January 1799 on the subject of an union. Dublin: printed for James Moore, 1799. Dublin: printed for James Moore, 1799. 93-166pp.

RLM: PA 739/5

Note: this copy evidently circulated separately from the Report of the debate on 22nd and

23rd January (R 13) with which its content has in all other inspected copies been associated.

R16 A report of the debate in the House of Commons of Ireland on Wednesday and Thursday the 15th and 16th of January 1800 on an amendment to the address moved by Sir Laurence Parsons, bart on the subject of an union. [The drop title is The parliamentary register.] Dublin: printed for James Moore, 1800. 142pp.

BLACK 2265   TCD: Gall Z 1 95 (1) • RIA: HP 806/11 (T-p signed
                    'Penelope Ball' in early 19th c. hand.) • RIA: HT 341/1
              NLI: P 619/5 • BL: 287 g 14 (5) • Bod: G Pamphlets 1967/7
                    CUL: Hib. 5. 800. 37 (1) • CUL: Hib. 5. 800. 38
                  CUL: Acton d 25 1070 (2) • CUL: Acton d 25 1070 (3)

R17 A report of the debate in the House of Commons of Ireland on Wednesday and Thursday the 5th and 6th of February 1800 on delivering a message from his majesty on an union. Dublin: printed for J Moore, 1800. 143-254pp.

BLACK 2264   RIA: HT 335/4 • NLI: P 619/6 • BL: 287 g 14 (6)
                    Bod: G Pamphlets 1967/9 • CUL: Hib. 5. 800. 37 (2)

R18 A report of the debate in the House of Commons of Ireland on Wednesday and Thursday the 5th and 6th of February 1800 on the king's message recommending a legislative union with Great Britain containing the propositions, also petitions from the city and county of Dublin, city of Limerick, the counties of Wexford, Limerick, Cavan, Meath, Tipperary, Longford, Monaghan, Kilkenny, Galway, and town of Belfast; with a list of the majority and minority. Dublin: printed by J Milliken, 1800. 94pp.

                  TCD: Crofton 209/12 • RIA: HT 337/6 • NLI: P 619/7

Dublin: printed by J Milliken and J Rice, 1800. 94pp.

                  CUL: Hib. 7. 88. 15 • CUL: Hib. 5. 800. 40

Dublin: printed by J Stockdale, 1800. 94pp.

                  CUL: Hib. 5. 798 (20)

R19 A report of the debate of the Irish bar on Sunday the 9th of December 1798 on the subject of an union of the legislatures of Great Britain and Ireland, to which is added the resolutions and protest. Dublin: printed for J Moore, 1799. 90pp.

Note: half-title of RIA: HT 330/9 bears ms note which reads 'said to have been taken down with particular care & corrected'. In RIA: HT 766/15 a ms alteration to list on p. [3] substitutes Pendleton in place of Rudleton.

BLACK 2148   TCD: V h 22 no. 2 • TCD: Crofton 182/14
                  TCD: Crofton 202/11 • TCD: Lecky A 4 32 no. 17
                    RIA: 766/ 15. • RIA: HT 330/9 • NLI: P 221/13
              NLI: P 251/17 • NLI: 619/3 • DCPL: Gilbert 15 B 34

BL: 8145 de 8 (8) • BL: 1509/523 (10) • Bod: G Pamphlets 2758/12
CUL: Hib. 5. 799. 88 • CUL: Hib. 5. 799. 89 • CUL: Hib. 7. 799. 37

R20 A report of the important debate in the House of Commons of Ireland on
Thursday April 11 1799 on the regency bill, including the admirable speech of
the right hon. John Foster (speaker). Dublin: printed by Campbell and Shea,
1799. 48pp.

Note: on union, see pp. 6, 8, 9, 18-19 et passim.

RIA: HP 779/6 • BL: 1508/1508

R21 A report of the important debate in the House of Commons of Ireland on
Thursday April 11 1799 on the regency bill, including an authentic copy of the
speech of the right hon. John Foster. Dublin: printed for J Moore, 1799. 12pp.

Note: this was evidently published to supplement, and physically to accompany, the
Moore edition (144pp.) of Foster's speech; nowhere in the 12pp is Foster quoted. See S 32
below, and cf. R 20 above for a rival solution to the problem.

RIA: HP 779/5 • BL: 287 g 14 (3)

R22 Report of the speech of Charles Ball esq in the House of Commons on
Wednesday May 21 1800 on the question of the union. Dublin: printed by
William Porter, 1800. 44pp.

TCD: Crofton 180 (8) • RIA: HT 336/16 • NLI: JP 3350
NLI: 607/7 (t-p damaged)

R23 A report of two speeches delivered by the rt. hon. lord viscount Castlereagh
in the debate on the regency bill on April 11th 1799. Dublin: printed by
Graisberry & Campbell for J Milliken, 1799. 34pp.

Date: Milliken ad. DJ 25 / 5/ 99 p. 2 col 1. ('A correct report ...')
Note: see p. 13 onwards re union.

TCD: Lecky A 4 36 (6) • TCD: Crofton 207/3 (*Tracts on the Union* vol 6)
RIA: HT 310/8 • NLI: I 6551 Dublin (1799) 20 • RLM: PA 739/7
BL: 104 c 25 (12)

Cork: printed by George Cherry, 1799. 32pp.

NLI: I 6551 Cork 1799 (7)

R24 Report on the events and circumstances which produced the union of the
kingdoms of England and Scotland; on the effect of this great national event on
the reciprocal interests of both kingdoms, and on the political and commercial
influence of Great Britain in the balance of power in Europe. [With appendix]
[London: printed for private distribution, 1799.] 2 vols - 404 and dxciii pp.

Format: no title-page as such appears in either vol. The 2nd vol, paged in small roman numerals with the concluding leaves (folding plates) foliated rather than paged, constitutes the appendix.

Authorship: John Bruce, 1745-1826 (attributed in Bodley) prepared the work for William Henry Cavendish Bentinck, third duke of Portland (1738-1809) who had been lord lieutenant of Ireland in 1782, and was prime minister of the united kingdom, 1807-09.

Note: The status of this work can be judged by the elegant full-leather binding and gilt edges of the State Paper Office copy (BL: 287 f 3-4). BL: 601 e 12-13 is the duke of Portland's copy, presented to him by Bruce, and subsequently by the Bentinck family to the British Museum. The CUL and TCD copies are similarly endorsed by Bruce.

TCD: M g 4-5 BL: 601 e 12-13 • BL: 287 f 3-4
Bod: Mason E 90 • CUL: Acton C 25 503-504

R25 Resolutions of the two houses of parliament of Ireland respecting a union of the kingdoms of Great Britain and Ireland and their address thereupon to his majesty. [Dublin, 1800.] 18pp.

Date-line: Ordered to be printed 2d April 1800.

BL: T 926 (17) • Bod: G Pamphlets 1677/15

R26 Rev Arthur O'Leary's address to the lords spiritual and temporal of the parliament of Great Britain, to which is annexed an account of Sir Henry Mildmay's bill relative to nuns. London: printed by Sampson Low for J [sic] Booker, 1800. [4] 66pp.

Date: 30 June 1800, according to M. B. Buckley in his *Life and Writings of ... O'Leary* (Dublin, 1868), p. 371.
Note: re. union see pp. 4-6, 10 etc. on the writer's motivation.

RLM: PA 30/4 • BL: 3942 aaa14

[a different impression which has no half-title] London: printed by Sampson Low for E [sic] Booker, 1800. [2] 66pp.

Note: this copy contains ms. alterations (p. 63).

Senate House Library (Univ. of London): Porteus

[Dublin]: London printed and Dublin reprinted by H Fitzpatrick, 1800. 44pp.

Note: this was issued in two states which are not identical settings of the type, with different addresses for Fitzpatrick: BL copies represent both states, the earlier being 4446 e 14 (6) from No 2 Up Ormond Quay; the later from No 4 Capel Street.

KID: 52/4 • BL: 4446 e 14 (6) • BL: 1568/1939

second edition. [Dublin]: London printed and Dublin reprinted by H Fitzpatrick, 1800. 44pp.

RIA: HP 797/1 • NLI: JP 219

Edinburgh: printed by J Moir and sold by Archibald MacDonald, 1800. 44pp.

Heythrop College Library (London): AC 900 Box/res

Cork: printed by George Cherry, 1800. 24pp.

NLI: I 6551 Cork 1800 (15)

R27 A review of Mr Grattan's Answer to the earl of Clare's speech. Part the first in which the merits of the constitution of 1782 and its aptness to the circumstances of Ireland are investigated. Dublin: printed for J Milliken, 1800. 34pp.

Authorship: A ms note on the flyleaf of TCD: Crofton 190 assigns the ninth item therein to 'Theobd. M'Kenna Esq.' According to the collective title-page of the volume (*Tracts on ... an union ... vol the ninth*), the ninth item is *A review of Mr Grattan's Answer ....* However, the volume does not contain a copy of this, a feature not wholly unusual among Milliken's packaged union tracts. The item actually placed ninth is *Memoirs of Francis Dobbs*, which cannot be plausibly assigned to M'Kenna. Consequently, the ms. note should be read as referring to the present item, the annotator responding to the collective contents page.

BLACK 2267   RIA: HP 797/6 • RIA: HP 805/3

R28 Review of a publication entitled The speech of the right honourable John Foster speaker of the House of Commons of Ireland, in a letter addressed to him. By William Smith. Dublin: printed and sold by Marchbank, 1799. 64pp.

Date: 'This day is published' (DJ 2/5/99 p. 2 col 1.)
Authorship: Sir William Cusack Smith - title-page.

BLACK 2164   TCD: Gall. P 25 52 (7) • RIA: HT 330/13 (t-p annotation
                          'by the author'.) • RIA: HT 336/27 (second item,
                     with book-seller's label) • NLI: P 155/2 • NLI: JP 4851
        CUL: Hib. 5. 799. 96 • CUL: Hib. 5. 799. 97 • CUL: Hib. 7. 799. 46

second edition. Dublin: printed and sold by Marchbank, 1799. 64pp.

NLI: P 1063/8 • NLI: P 615/2 • RIA: HT 330/6 • BL: 1104 c 25 (11)

third edition. Dublin: printed and sold by Marchbank, 1799. 64pp.

Date-line, p. 63, April 27th 1799. • TCD: Crofton 207/4

RIA: HP 786/ 9 • RIA: HT 311/10 • RIA: HT 332/17 • BL: 8145 dd 68

a new edition. [London:] Dublin printed; London reprinted [by S Gosnell] for J Wright, 1799. 96pp.

CUL: Hib. 5. 798. 2/2 • BL: 117 h 26

R29 A review of the question of union in July 1799 [drop title, no preliminaries] 122pp.

Authorship: The original owner of RLM: PA 870/1 inscribed the first page 'Written by Edward Cooke, Esq. Under Secretary in the Civil Depart. but never published - '

Note: Two different systems of leading are employed, and one or two 'pages' are inserted in the form of printed slips; last page unnumbered. This item probably represents proofs of an abandoned project. Only the one copy listed has been located.

RLM: PA 870/1

R30 A review of the speech of the right hon. William Pitt in the British House of Commons on Thursday January 31 1799. By Robert Orr. Dublin: printed by J Stockdale, 1799. 48pp.

Authorship: Robert Orr (title-page).
Note: refers, p. 1, to 'the gratuitous distribution of [Pitt's speech] by the King's printer'.

BLACK 2135   TCD: 91 p 38 no. 11 (t-p ms note – 'To Charles Bushe esq from the author': errata on p. 48. • TCD: Crofton 205/13 RIA: HT 312/6 • RIA: HT 313/4 • RIA: HT 331/19 (incomplete) NLI: JP 3344 • CUL: Hib. 5. 798. 68 (5)

R31 The rights of the imperial crown of Ireland asserted and maintained against Edward Cooke, Esq., reputed author of a pamphlet entitled "Arguments for and against an union, etc" in a letter to that gentleman. By George Barnes. Dublin: printed for W Gilbert, 1799. 96pp.

Date: date-line, p. 96, December 17th 1798.
Authorship: George Barnes – title-page.
Note: a printed PS provides details of printing schedule. RIA: HT 319/9 is a presentation copy from the author to the bishop of Elphin. See also NLI: J 32341, a 3rd ed. of 1803 (lacks prelims) with extensive ms annotations re. linen industry etc.

BLACK 2049   TCD: V h 22 no. 9 • RIA: HP 767/8 • RIA: HT 319/9

second edition with additions. Dublin: printed for W. Gilbert, 1799. 100pp.

Date: an inscription on top leaf of RIA: HT 319/10, seemingly in the author's hand cf RIA: HT 319/9, reads '17 Decr. 1798'.

TCD: 91 p 38 no. 15 (T-p ms note – 'From the Author')
TCD: Lecky A 4 33 no. 3 • TCD: Crofton 203/3 • RIA: HT 315/5
RIA: HT 319/10 (bound in original blue papers) • RIA: HT 323/2
RIA: HT 325/8 • NLI: P 5/1 • NLI: P 607/9 ('From the Author' t-p ms.)
NLI: JP 3341 • NLI: I 6551 Dublin (1799) 50 • BL: 8143 d 3

S

S1 A second letter to the electors of Ireland on the projected measure of an union. By a freeholder. Dublin: printed for J Moore, 1799. 16pp.

Authorship: attributed to 'Mr Spencer' [ie Joshua Spencer] in ms note in TCD: Crofton 185.

BLACK 2156   TCD: V h 22 no. 15 • TCD: Crofton 185/2

TCD: Crofton 205/2 • RIA: HP 787/ 2 • RIA: HT 331/12
NLI: P 621/13 • RLM: PA 867/3 (with half-title) • BL: 1509/1148

S2 A second letter to the right honorable William Pitt. Dublin: printed by George Folingsby, 1799. 50pp.

Date: 28th February 1799 (date-line, p. 50); 'On Monday morning at twelve o'clock [ie on 11/3/99] will be published' (DJ 9/3/99 p. 4 col 2).
Authorship: William Drennan (p. 50).

BLACK 2078   TCD: Crofton 182/16 • TCD: Gall Z 1 95 (5)
RIA: HP 786/ 1 • RIA: HT 333/4 • NLI: P 609/10
BL: 1509/888 • BL: 1509/1179

S3 The second part of Taaffe's reflections on the union. Dublin: printed by Joseph Mehain, 1799. 48pp.

Authorship: Dennis Taaffe.

BLACK 2170   TCD: V h 21 no. 9 • TCD: Lecky A 4 32 no. 9
RIA: HT 316/7 • RIA: HT 321/1

S4 A short address to the people of Ireland on the subject of an union. By a freeholder. Dublin: printed for William Jones, 1799. 24pp.
Date: 'This Day is Published' (DJ 10/1/99 p. 3 col. 4).

Authorship: attributed by implication to 'Mr Spencer' [ie Joshua Spencer] in a ms note in TCD: Crofton 185.

BLACK 2160   TCD: V h 23 no. 14 • RIA: HP 787/ 4 • NLI: P 621/11
BL: 8145 de 8 (1)

S5 Sketch of financial and commercial affairs in the autumn of 1797. The fourth edition to which is added a supplement containing some observations on the proposed union with Ireland etc etc. written early in the spring of 1799. By Sir Robert Herries. London: printed for J Wright, 1799. 146pp.

Authorship: Sir Robert Herries (1730-1815) - title-page.

BLACK 1963 (lists 1st ed, anon 1797, only)
University of Pennsylvania: 330. 8 P753 v 70

S6 A sketch of the most obvious causes of the poverty, ignorance, and general want of civilization amongst the peasantry of Ireland and a comparison between their situation and that of the peasantry of Great Britain, with a practicable plan for improving their manners and for making their circumstances more eligible than they have ever been, chiefly by a liberal attention to the education of the rising generation, and by the establishment of poor laws and taxes for their permanent relief; to which are added impartial strictures on the proposed legislative union between Ireland and Britain; questions relative to it and to the English minister, to a probable land tax, city of Dublin trade and manufactures, excess of our population, lawyers, attorneys, absentees, reduction of the rates of provisions, house and land rents, places, pensions etc. By a sincere friend to humanity, to peace, and the constitution. Dublin: printed for J Milliken, 1799. 36pp.

BLACK 2162   RIA: HT 316/11 • RIA: HT 331/17

S7 Sketches of Irish political characters of the present day shewing the parts they respectively take on the question of the union, what places they hold, their characters as speakers etc etc. London: printed for the author by T Davison, 1799. 312pp.

Authorship: Henry MacDougall - BL.
Note: the presence of an engraving of the 'New Royal Standard of Great Britain and Ireland', dated 1801, in BL: 10804 b 4 (title page date 1799) indicates that this item was re-issued perhaps two years after its original publication, or at least distribution in this form.

BLACK 2119   TCD: Gall NN 19. 51 • BL: 1453 f 1 (1) • BL: 10804 b 4
                                                      CUL: Hib. 5. 799. 94

S8 Some observations on the projected union between Great Britain and Ireland and the inexpediency of agitating the measure at this time. By J H C. Dublin: printed by Wm M'Kenzie, 1798. 36pp.

Authorship: James Henry Cottingham; author's surname given on the printed title-page of Milliken's collective *Tracts on ... Union* (vol 2); attributed to James Henry Cottingham in a ms note on RIA: HP 767/1; NLI concurs.

TCD: V h 22 no. 6 • TCD: Lecky A 4 33 no. 1 • TCD: Crofton 203/1
RIA: HP 767/ 1 • NLI: P 2/13 • NLI: P 128/5 • NLI: 251/11
BL: 8145 de 11 (4) • Bod: Vet A5 e 6027

S9 Some observations on an union being a continuation of letters lately published from a gentleman in the county of Cork to his friend in Bath. Cork: printed at the Herald-office, 1799. 12pp.

RIA: HT 321/3

S10 Some strictures on the conduct of administration during the session of parliament that opened under Charles, marquis Cornwallis, on the 22d of January and closed on the 1st of June 1799. Dublin: printed by J Milliken, 1800. 54pp.

RIA: HP 796/7 • RLM: PA 872/3

S11 The speech (at length) of the honourable Henry Grattan in the Irish House of Commons against the union with Great Britain. London: printed by A Paris for J. S. Jordan, 1800. 36pp.

Authorship: Henry Grattan (1746-1820) - title-page.

BLACK 2231   CUL: Hib. 5. 800. 34

London: printed by A Paris for J S Jordan and sold by J Smith and by all the booksellers at the Royal Exchange, 1800. 36pp.

RIA: HP 797/4 • BL: T 137 (6) • CUL: Hib. 800. 33
Bod: G Pamphlets 197/3

S12 The speech delivered by Doctor Duigenan in the House of Commons of Ireland, February 5 1800, on the subject of an incorporating union with Great Britain, earnestly recommended to the serious consideration of the loyal citizens of Dublin. Dublin: printed by Rea, 1800. 24pp.

Authorship: Patrick Duigenan (1735-1816) - title-page.

RIA: HP 795/5 • RIA: HP 806/2
NLI: P 609/12 (prelims untrimmed; text on untrimmed smaller pages)
BL 8145 cc 18 • Bod: G Pamphlets 1207/3
CUL: Hib. 7. 800. 9

S13 A speech delivered by the right honourable John Foster in the committee on the regency bill, comprehending the question of an union. [Dublin]; printed by T Henshall, 1799. 20pp.

University of Illinois (Urbana - Champaign): x941.57. Or4sp

S14 The speech of Arthur Moore, esq. delivered in the Irish House of Commons on Thursday the 13th of March 1800 on the motion that an humble address be presented to his majesty praying that he may be graciously pleased to dissolve the present parliament and call a new one before any final arrangement shall be concluded upon relative to the measure of a legislative union. Dublin: printed by J Moore, 1800. 28pp.

Authorship: Arthur Moore - title-page.

RIA: HT 335/6 • NLI: JP 3349 • BL: 287 g 14 (9)

S15 The speech of Henry Grattan esq. on the subject of a legislative union with Great Britain; the resolutions of the Roman Catholics of the city of Dublin, the guild of merchants, the freemen and freeholders of the city of Dublin at an aggregate meeting held on the 16th of January last; the celebrated speech delivered on that occasion by John Philpot Curran esq. and the resolutions of the county of Dublin etc etc. Dublin: printed by J Stockdale, 1800. 32pp.

Authorship: Henry Grattan (1746-1820) - title-page.

BLACK 2232   RIA: HP 806/ 12 • NLI: P 612/1 • NLI: JP 3348
BL: 8145 b 49 • CUL: Hib. 5. 798. 68 (16)

S16 The speech of the honourable George Knox, representative in parliament for the University of Dublin in the House of Commons, February 17 1800, on the subject of an incorporate union of Great Britain and Ireland. London: printed [by S Gosnell] for J Debrett, 1800. 20pp.

Authorship: George Knox - title-page.

Bod: 8 Y 84/4 Jur.

S17 Speech of Lord Hawkesbury in the House of Commons Friday April 25th 1800 on the incorporation of the parliaments of Great Britain and Ireland. London: printed for J Wright, 1800. 36pp (inc. ads.)

Authorship: Charles Jenkinson (1727-1808) – title-page.

RIA: HT 335/7 • RIA: HT 337/5 (lacks ads.) • RLM: PA 875/3 (lacks ads.)
CUL: Hib. 5. 800. 44 • CUL: Hib. 5. 800. 45 • CUL: Hib. 7. 800. 21

S18 The speech of Lord Minto in the House of Peers, April 11 1799, on a motion for an address to his majesty to communicate the resolutions of the two houses of parliament respecting an union between Great Britain and Ireland. Dublin: printed by John Exshaw, 1799. 156pp.

Date: 'This Day is published' (DJ 21/5/99 p. 3 col. 1.)
Authorship: Gilbert Elliot (1751-1814), first earl of Minto - title-page.

TCD: Lecky A 4 36 (7) • TCD: Crofton 207/8 • RIA: HP 788/1
RIA: HT 318/3 • RIA: HT 329/2 (second item) • RIA: HT 329/3
RIA: HT 330/15 • NLI: P 153/4 • NLI: P 212/5 • NLI: JP 4858
BL: 1103 g 9 (1) • BL: 1104 c 25 (7) • Bod: 22955 3 31
CUL: Hib. 5. 799. 63 • CUL: Hib. 5. 799. 64 • CUL: Hib. 5. 799. 65

London: printed for John Stockdale, 1799. 156pp.

NLI: P 103/5 • RLM: PA 1129/5 • BL: 709 (6)
BL: 117 h 27 • BL: 111 d 62 • Bod: Vet A5 e 4995/2
CUL: Hib. 7. 799. 26 • CUL: Hib. 5. 799. 62

Cork: printed by George Cherry, 1799. 128pp.

NLI: I 6551 Cork 1799 (21)

S19 Speech of Patrick Duigenan esq LLD in the House of Commons of Ireland, February 5 1800 on his excellency the lord lieutenant's message on the subject of an incorporative union with Great Britain earnestly recommended to the serious consideration of the loyal citizens of Dublin. Dublin: printed for J Milliken, 1800. 28pp.

Authorship: Patrick Duigenan (1735-1816) - title-page.

BLACK 2214   TCD: Crofton 209/2 • RIA: HT 335/10
CUL: Hib. 5. 800. 18

S20 Speech of Patrick Duigenan LLD in the Irish House of Commons, Wednesday Feb 5 1800 on the subject of an incorporating union between Great-Britain and Ireland. London: printed [by T Bayliss] for J Wright, 1800. 50pp.

Date: CUL: Hib 5. 800. 19 title-page has ms. note giving 'Feby 17'; this is probably in the hand of John Wright, the publisher, or a person acting officially on his behalf.
Authorship: Patrick Duigenan (1735-1816) - title-page.
Note: CUL: Hib. 5. 800. 19 has half-title and, has bound at the end 8pp. of 'New publications printed for J Wright', the pp printed by T Bayliss. Between the conclusion of Duigenan and the advertisements a 2pp insert carries ms opinions on the text, quoted from magazines of the day. In the first 'the principal objections' against union are ascribed to 'the partizans of "Things as they are"'. This phrase constituting the alternative title of William Godwin's novel, *Caleb Williams* (1794), links anti-unionism to the politics of English radicals such as Godwin.

RLM: PA 874/4 • BL: 1103 k 7 • CUL: Hib. 5. 798. 1/5
CUL: Hib. 5. 800. 19

S21 Speech of Richard Brinsley Sheridan esq. in the House of Commons of Great Britain on Tuesday January 31st 1799 in reply to Mr Pitt's speech on the union with Ireland. Dublin: printed for James Moore, 1799. 26pp.

Authorship: Richard Brinsley Sheridan (1751-1816) - title-page.

BLACK 2159   TCD: V h 25 no. 14 • RIA: HP 787/ 13 • RIA: HT 331/4
(incomplete) • NLI: JP 3346 • BL: 1104 c 25 (2)

S22 The speech of Richard Martin esq. in the House of Commons on the 21st day of May 1800 on the motion that leave be given to bring in the union bill. Dublin: printed for B Dornin, 1800. 64pp.

Authorship: Richard 'Humanity Dick' Martin (1754-1834) - title-page.

BLACK 2246   RIA: HP 805/4 • RIA: HT 337/3

S23 The speech of the right honourable Barry, lord Yelverton, chief baron of his majesty's court of exchequer, in the House of Lords of Ireland on Saturday March 22 1800, in the debate on the fourth article of a legislative union between Great Britain and Ireland. Published by authority. Dublin: printed by J Milliken, 1800. 36pp.

Authorship: Barry Yelverton (1736-1805) - title-page.

BLACK 2192   TCD: Crofton 209/9 • RIA: HP 806/6 (top edges cropped)
RIA: HT 335/27 • NLI: P 107/9 • NLI: P 615/18 • BL: 8145 cc 111

The speech of the right honorable ... [London:] Dublin printed; London: reprinted [by T Gosnell] for J Wright , 1800. 36pp.

Date: BL: 117 h 41 half-title has ms additional note '22 March 1800' which may record date of publication, ie simultaneous with the speech in the Irish House of Lords.

RLM: PA 877/1 (without half-title)
BL: 117 h 41 (bound with 8pp 'New Publications'.

S24 Speech of the right honourable John Beresford, on his moving the sixth article of the union in the House of Commons of Ireland, March 19th 1800.

Authorship: John Claudius Beresford (1738-1805) - title-page.

third edition. Dublin: printed for J Milliken, 1800. 40pp.

TCD: Crofton 209/6 • NLI: P 607/11 (untrimmed)

S25 Speech of the right honourable John Beresford, on his moving the sixth article of the union in the House of Commons of Ireland, March 27th 1800. Dublin: printed for J Milliken, 1800. 40pp.

Authorship: John Claudius Beresford (1738-1805) - title-page.

BLACK 2196   RIA: HP 806/4 • NLI: P 607/10

second edition. Dublin: printed for J Milliken, 1800. 40pp.

RIA: HT 336/1 (partly uncut) • NLI: P 107/10
NLI: P 153/2 • NLI: P 155/4

third edition. Dublin: printed for J Milliken, 1800. 40pp.

RIA: HT 335/1

London: printed [by T Baylis] for J Wright, 1800. 40pp.

Date: the first listed of the CUL copies has 'April 11' inserted in ms in the t-p date, inscription by publisher.

RLM: PA 874/2 • BL: 117 h 42 • CUL: Hib. 5. 800. 5
CUL: Hib. 7.800. 3 • CUL: Hib. 5. 798. 1/8

S26 The speech of the right honourable John, earl of Clare, lord high chancellor of Ireland, in the House of Lords of Ireland, on a motion made by him on Monday February 10 1800. Dublin: printed by J Milliken, 1800. 104pp.

Authorship: John Fitzgibbon (1749-1802) - title-page.

BLACK 2204   RIA: HT 339/2 • NLI: P 119/7 • NLI: P 128/4
NLI: P 153/1 • NLI: P 212/13 • NLI: P 226/2 • NLI: P 608/4
CUL: Hib. 5. 800. 9 • CUL: Hib. 5. 800. 10
CUL: Hib. 5. 800. 11 • CUL: Hib. 7. 800. 5

second edition. Dublin: printed by J Milliken, 1800. 104pp.

RIA: HP 806/5 • RIA: HT 336/24 • RIA: HT 339/3
NLI: P 608/5 (untrimmed)
see also BL: 113 g 8 (2)

third edition. Dublin: printed by J Milliken, 1800. 104pp.

RIA: HT 339/1 • NLI: P 608/6

fifth edition. Dublin: printed by J Milliken, 1800. 96pp surviving.

RIA: HT 337/(unnumbered)

sixth edition. Dublin: printed by J Milliken, 1800. 104pp.

TCD: Crofton 209/7

seventh edition. Dublin: printed by J Milliken, 1800. 104pp.

NLI: P 401/8 • CUL: Hib. 5. 800. 12 • CUL: Hib. 5. 800. 13

[London:] Dublin printed; London: re-printed for J Wright, 1800. 104pp.

RLM: PA 1130/5 • CUL: Hib. 5. 800. 14 .
CUL: Hib. 7. 800. 6 • CUL: Hib. 5. 798. 1/7

S27 Speech of the right honorable John Foster, speaker of the House of
Commons of Ireland, delivered in committee on Monday the 17th day of
February, 1800. Dublin: printed for James Moore, 1800. 44pp. + 1 folding table
+ 1p. of statistics.

Authorship: John Foster (1740-1828) - title-page.

BLACK 2226   TCD: Crofton 209/3 • RIA: HP 806/3 • RIA: HT 335/12
RIA: HT 336/27 (first item) • NLI: P 119/6 • NLI: P 226/4
NLI: P 610/9 • NLI: JP 3347 • RLM: PA 871/5 • BL: 1103 g 8 (3)
BL: 287 g 14 (7) • Bod: Vet A 5 e 6145 (2) • Bod: G Pamphlets 1967/6 •
CUL: Hib. 5. 800. 56 • CUL: Hib. 5. 800. 57

Dublin: printed by J Stockdale, 1800. 24pp.

RIA: HT 336/5 • NLI: JP 874

Cork: printed by James Haly, 1800. 30pp. + folding statistics (2).

NLI: JP 894

(honourable ... House ofc [sic] Ommons [sic] ...). [London:] Dublin printed:
London: reprinted for J Debrett by A Wilson, 1800. 60pp.

RIA: HT 338/1 • RLM: PA 1130/9 • CUL: Hib. 5. 800. 58
CUL: Hib. 5. 800. 59

S28 {The union} Speech of the right honorable John Foster speaker of the
House of Commons of Ireland delivered in a committee on Monday the 17th of
February 1800, to which is added the celebrated speech of William Saurin esq on
Friday the 21st of February 1800 on a legislative union with Great Britain.
Dublin: printed for J Moore, 1800. 16 + folding table + 8 pp.

Authorship: John Foster (1740-1828) - title-page.

RIA: HT 336/27
NLI: P 611/4 • CUL: Hib. 5. 800. 56 • CUL: Hib. 5. 800. 57

honourable ... [London:] Dublin printed; London reprinted for J Debrett by A
Wilson, 1800. 58pp.

CUL: Hib. 5. 800. 58 (with half-title-page)
CUL: Hib. 5. 800. 59 (without half-title-page)

S29 Speech of the right honorable John Foster speaker of the House of
Commons of Ireland delivered in committee on Wednesday the 19th of March
1800. Dublin: printed for J Moore, 1800. 38pp.

Date: RLM: PA 871/1 title-page bears owner's [ie George Watson's] inscription "From
the Speaker April 10 [? or 18?] th. G. W."
Authorship: John Foster (1740-1828) - title-page.

BLACK 2227   TCD: Crofton 209/4 • RIA: HT 335/11 • RLM: PA 871/1
BL: 287 g 14 (10) • CUL: Hib. 5. 800. 61

S30 Speech of the right honorable John Foster, speaker of the House of
Commons of Ireland, delivered in committee of the whole house on Thursday the
11th day [sic] of April 1799. Dublin: printed for James Moore, 1799. 46pp.

Authorship: John Foster (1740-1828) - title-page.

TCD: Lecky A 4 36 (3) • NLI: P 212/6 • NLI: P 379/4
NLI: P 611/3 • CUL: Hib. 5. 799. 76

S31 Speech of the right honorable John Foster, speaker of the House of
Commons of Ireland, delivered in committee of the whole house on Thursday the
11th [sic] of April 1799. London: printed for G G and J Robinson, 1799. 112pp.

Authorship: John Foster (1740-1828) - title-page.
Note: Most copies have an errata list p. [iii]; Bod: G Pamphlets 1966/7 has both ms.
corrections and errata list p. [iii].

NLI: P 611/1 • RLM: PA 577/3 • CUL: Hib. 5. 799. 77
(untrimmed, with half-title-page) • CUL: Hib. 5. 799. 78
CUL: Hib. 5. 798. 1 (9) • Bod: G Pamphlets 1966/7

S32 Speech of the right honorable John Foster, speaker of the House of
Commons of Ireland, delivered in committee on Thursday the 11th day [sic] of
April 1799. Dublin: printed by James Moore, 1799. 114pp.

Authorship: John Foster (1740-1828) - title-page.
Notes: (i) The printing history of this item awaits its chronicler; both as to title-page
ornament and substantive text, there are variants. The CUL copies differ in title-page
ornament - nos. 7. 799. 34 and 5. 799. 72 having a single rule where the others have
double. Moreover, 7. 799. 32 has an errata list on a p. [115], whereas the other four CUL
copies have no such page.
    Among BL copies, 8146 ee 23 (10) has no errata list though the last of the errata

provided in 1103 g 9 (3) appears to have been adopted in the former. Bod: G Pamphlets 1966/8 may be a very early state as it has no errata list and the last errata (as given in BL: 1103 g 9 (3) has not been adopted. This particular detail, revolving round the use of the word 'treason', clearly was sensitive.

(ii) BL: 1103 g 9 (3) has a contemporary newspaper cutting re. correspondence between Portland and Shelburne in 1782.

BLACK 2087 (one edition cited only)   TCD: Gall. Z 1 95 (2)
TCD: Crofton 207/2 • RIA: HP 788/3 • RIA: HT 320/4
NLI: P 103/4 • NLI: P 155/1 • NLI: P 611/2 • NLI: JP 341
RLM: PA 871/2 • RLM: PA 1045/6 • BL: 1103 g 9 (3)
BL: 8146 ee 23 (10) • BL: 1104 c 25 (10) • BL: 287 g 14 (3)
CUL: Hib. 7. 799. 32 • CUL: Hib. 7. 799. 33 • CUL: Hib. 7. 799. 34
CUL: Hib. 5. 799. 72 • CUL: Hib. 5. 799. 73
Bod: G Pamphlets 1966/8 • Bod: Vet A5 e 6145/1

[same title] Dublin: printed by James Moore, 1799. 144pp.

Note: this was evidently distributed, at least in a substantial number of instances, in a form allowing R21 to act in effect as its prelims., for the title-page of that publication claims to include an authentic copy [sic] of Foster's speech. At least some examples, e.g. that in BL, wrongly give 'Mr Rochfort' on p. 3 as the person speaking.

NLI: P 610/8 (errata p. [143]) • BL: 287 g 14 (3) 2nd item thereof

[same title] Dublin: printed for James Moore, 1799. 48pp.

RIA: HT 323/1 • RIA: HT 331/2

[same title] Dublin: printed for James Moore, 1799. 38pp.

NLI: P 610/10 (untrimmed)

[same title] London: printed for G G & J Robinson, 1799. 112pp.

BL: T 95 (3) • BL: 8146 ee 23 (10) • BL: 111 d 57
BL: 117 h 24 • Bod: G Pamphlets 1966/7

[S33 number deleted]

S34 The speech of the right hon Arthur Lord Kilwarden lord chief justice of the King's Bench and late one of the representatives in parliament for the city of Dublin as delivered in the House of Lords of Ireland, Monday Feb 10, 1800, recommended to the perusal of the citizens of Dublin. Dublin: printed for J Milliken, 1800. 16pp.

Authorship: Arthur Wolfe (1739-1803) - title-page.

RIA: HT 336/6 (uncut) • BL: 8145 cc 110 • CUL: Hib. 7. 800. 18

S35 The speech of the right honourable lord viscount Carleton chief justice of the court of common pleas in the House of Lords of Ireland on Monday the 10th of February 1800 on the following resolution – that in order to promote and secure the essential interests of Great Britain and Ireland and to consolidate the strength, power and resources of the British empire it will be adviseable to concur in such measures as may best tend to unite the two kingdoms of Great Britain and Ireland into one kingdom in such a manner and on such terms and conditions as may be established by acts of the respective parliaments of Great Britain and Ireland. Dublin: printed by John Exshaw, 1800. 34pp.

Authorship: Hugh Carleton (1739-1826) - title-page.

RIA: HT 335/13 • RIA: HT 335/21 • RIA: HT 336/18
CUL: Hib. 5. 800. 7

S36 Speech of the right honourable lord viscount Castlereagh in the Irish House of Commons, Wednesday February 5 1800, on offering to the House certain resolutions proposing and recommending a complete and entire union between Great Britain and Ireland. London: printed [by T Gosnell] for J Wright, 1800. 72pp.

Authorship: Robert Stewart (1769-1822) - title-page.

RIA: HT 337/2 • NLI: P 119/8 • BL: T 137 (2)
Bod: Johnson d 563 • CUL: Hib. 5. 798. 1 (6)

S37 [T]he speech of the right honorable lord viscount Castlereagh upon delivering to the House of Commons of Ireland his excellency the lord lieutenant's message on the subject of an incorporating union with Great Britain, with the resolutions; containing the terms on which it is proposed to carry that measure in effect, February 5 1800. Dublin: printed by J Rea, 1800. 56pp.

Authorship: Robert Stewart (1759-1822) - title-page.
Note: The initial letter of the first word is missing in early copies (e.g. CUL: Hib. 7. 800. 23)

BLACK 2201   TCD: Gall. P 25 52 (3) • RIA: HP 806/ 1 • RIA: HT 336/23
NLI: P 153/7 • NLI: P 128/3 • NLI: P 608/2 • BL: 8145 cc 101
CUL: Hib. 5. 800. 46 • CUL: Hib. 5. 800. 47 • CUL: Hib. 5. 800. 48
CUL: Hib. 7. 800. 22 • CUL: Hib. 7. 800. 23 • Bod: Vet A 5 e 6145 (3)

honourable ... Dublin: printed by J Milliken, 1800. 60pp.

TCD: Crofton 209/1 • NLI: P 226/1 • BL: 8135 ccc 1 (7)

third editon corrected. London: printed [by T. Gillet] for John Stockdale, 1800. 46, [10]pp.

BL: 08139 ccc 48 (5)

S38 Speech of the right honourable Sylvester Douglas in the House of Commons, Tuesday April the 23d 1799, on seconding the motion of the right honourable the chancellor of the exchequer for the house to agree with the Lords in an address to his majesty relative to a union with Ireland. London: printed for

J Wright, 1799. 196pp.

Date: CUL copy of the 2nd ed. has 'Sep 5' annotation of imprint date.
Authorship: Sylvester Douglas (title-page), baron Glenbervie.
BLACK 2093, 2229   TCD: Lecky A 3 25 (4) • RIA: HP 788/ 7
              NLI: P 609/8 • BL: C T 238 (2) • CUL: Hib. 7. 799. 11
           (with errata slip) • CUL: Hib. 7. 799. 12 • CUL: Hib. 7. 799. 33

second edition. London: printed [by S Gosnell] for J Wright, 1800. 204pp.

Note: includes index, pp. 197-204, some copies also have an errata slip between p. 196 and
p. 197. Bod: Vet A5 d 885 (no errata slip) is the author's presentation copy to Lord Minto.

      RIA: HT 335/5 • RIA: HT 324/4 (second item) • CUL: Hib. 5. 800. 78

                     Bod: 22956 d 14 • Bod: Vet A5 d 885

Dublin: printed for John Milliken, 1799. 196pp.

Date: 'This Day is published' (DJ 1/10/99 p. 3 col 2.)

          TCD: Crofton 207/6 • NLI: P 379/6 • NLI: P 609/7

                     RLM: PA 875/6 • BL: 8145 d 18

S39 The speech of the right hon. William Pitt in the British House of Commons
on Thursday January 31 1799. Dublin: printed by George Grierson, 1799. 54pp.

Authorship: William Pitt (1759-1806) - title-page.
Note: ESTC notes two variants of punctuation of the date cited in the title. See Robert
Orr's *Review of the speech of ... Pitt* [p. 1] for ref to this pamphlet's 'gratuitous distribution
... by the King's printer', ie Grierson.

BLACK 2138   TCD: V h 25 no. 13 • TCD: Crofton 207/4
       TCD: Gall Z 1 95 (3) • RIA: HP 787/ 17 • RIA: HT 305/7 (2nd item)
      RIA: HT 312/1 • RIA: HT 312/4 • RIA: HT 312/5 • RIA: HT 317/15
        RIA: HT 333/8 • NLI: P 93/9 • NLI: P 212/1 • NLI: P 221/17
           BL: 1490 p 107 • BL: 1560/3914 (11) • BL: 1560/481
      Bod: 8 Y 83/16 Jur. • Bod: Vet A5 e 2977/1 • CUL: Hib. 5. 799. 85
              CUL: Hib. 5. 799. 86 • CUL: Hib. 7. 799. 35

See also NLI: P 153/5 for a 30pp. ed. which lacks its title-page, with the
consequence that the title or imprint cannot be established from the evidence
here available.

S40 Speech of the right honourable William Pitt in the House of Commons,
Thursday January 31 1799, on offering to the House the resolutions which he
proposed as the basis of an union between Great Britain and Ireland. London:
printed for J Wright, 1799. 96pp.

Authorship: William Pitt (1759-1806) - title-page.

          RIA: HT 315/6 • RIA: HT 321/7 • BL: 8145 c 66
      BL: 111 d 67 • Bod: Vet A5 d 661 • Bod: Johnson d 553
                     CUL: Hib. 5. 799. 83

third edition. London: printed for J Wright, 1799. 96pp.

CUL: Hib. 7. 799. 36

fifth edition. London: printed for J Wright, 1799. 96pp.

NLI: P 119/4

sixth edition. London: printed for J Wright, 1799. 96pp.

RIA: HT 323/5 • RLM: PA 1129/1 • BL: T 137 (5)

eighth edition. London: printed for J Wright, 1799. 96pp.

RLM: PA 875/1 • CUL: Hib. 5. 799. 84

S41 Speech of the right honourable William Pitt in the House of Commons Thursday January 31 1799, on offering to the House the resolutions which he proposed as the basis of an union between Great Britain and Ireland, to which are added the speeches of the right honourable John Foster on the 12th and 15th of August 1785 on the bill for effectuating the intercourse and commerce between Great Britain and Ireland on permanent and equitable principles for the mutual benefit of both kingdoms. Dublin: printed by John Exshaw, 1799. 122pp.

Date: 'At one o'clock this Day will be published' (DJ Saturday 16/2/99 p. 1 col. 3)
Authorship: William Pitt (1759-1806) and John Foster (1740-1828) - title-page.

BLACK 2139   RIA: HT 320/5 • RIA: HT 322/14 • RIA: HT 323/6
RIA: HT 332/14 (incomplete) • BL: 1103 g 9 (2) • BL: 1560/431
BL: 1560/3914 (11) • BL: 1490 p 107 • Bod: G Pamphlets 1205/2

[same imprint] 116pp.

BL: 1104 c 25 (1) • BL: 1103 g 9 (2) • Bod: G Pamphlets 1205/2

S42 The speech of Thomas Goold esquire in the Irish House of Commons, February 14 1800 on the subject of an incorporate union of Great Britain and Ireland. London: printed for J Debrett by Wilson and Co, 1800. 40pp.

Authorship: Thomas Goold (1766?-1846) - title-page.

RIA: HT 335/9 • RLM: PA 1130/6 • BL: 1608/ 3680
CUL: Hib. 5. 800. 35

S43 Speech of William Johnson esq on the regency bill in the House of Commons on the 18th day of April 1799. Dublin: printed for J Milliken, 18pp.

Authorship: William Johnson - title-page.
Note: while denying that he is dealing with a union proposition, the author proceeds to discuss it several times (see pp. 3, 15 etc.)

RIA: HP 779/4

S44 Speeches delivered in the House of Lords of Ireland by John, earl of Clare, lord high chancellor of Ireland; viz I, Speech on the second reading of the bill for the relief of his majesty's Roman Catholic subjects, March 13 1793: II, Speech on a motion made by the earl of Moira for the adoption of such conciliatory measures as may allay misapprehensions and discontents in Ireland, February 19 1798: III, Speech on taking his majesty's message into consideration relative to a legislative union between Great Britain and Ireland, February 10 1800; to which is added, The speech of the right hon. John Foster, speaker of the House of Commons in the committee on the Roman Catholic bill, February 27 1793. Dublin: printed for J Milliken, 1800. [2], 42, 24, 84, 104pp.

Authorship: John Fitzgibbon (1749-1802) and John Foster (1740-1828) - title-page.
Note: this is a composite publication, physically incorporating earlier pamphlets, with a collective t-p added. CUL: Hib. 5. 800. 77 (incomplete) contains only matter issued originally under Marchbank's imprint.

NLI: P 608/7 • BL: RB 23 a 2022

S45 Strictures on a pamphlet entitled Arguments for and against an union between Great Britain and Ireland considered. Dublin: printed by William Porter, 1798. 24pp.

Date: T-p ms note 'Published about 16 Dec' in NLI: P 620/3; t-p ms. note reads 'pubd 16 Decr' in RIA: HP 766/13.
Authorship: Both BL and Bod attribute to John Humfrey, of Dublin. TCD: Crofton 182 fly-leaf list attributes it to 'Mr Humphreys, Atty'. Black concurs. Author's name given on the title-page of the second edition.
BLACK 2008, 2099   TCD: V h 21 no. 10 • TCD: Crofton 182/13
RIA: HP 766/ 13 • NLI: P 251/8 • NLI: P 620/3
BL: 8145 de 9 (4) • Bod: G. Pamphlet 1965 (2)

By John Humfrey. Second edition with additions and corrections. Dublin: printed by William Porter, 1799. 32pp.

TCD: Lecky A 4 32 no. 16 • RIA: HT 327/9 • NLI: Ir. 9107 p 14 (5)

S46 Strictures on the proposed union between Great-Britain and Ireland, with occasional remarks. By Nicholas Gay. Dublin: printed by John Exshaw, 1799. 40pp.

Date: 'just published' (DJ 15/10/99 p. 1 col 3.)
Authorship: Nicholas Gay, FRS - title-page.
BLACK 2089   RIA: HT 318/7 • NLI: Ir 94107 p 14 (1) • BL: 1509/874.
Bod: G Pamphlets 2758/13

London: printed [by T Gillet] for John Stockdale, 1799. 40pp • BL: B 505 (5)

BL: 117 h 29 • CUL: Hib. 5. 799. 159

second edition. London: printed [by T Gillet] for J Stockdale, 1800. 42pp.

Note: The second London edition is re-set.

CUL: Hib. 5. 800. 28

S47 Strictures upon the union betwixt Great Britain and Ireland. By an officer. Dublin: printed for Bernard Dornin, 1798. 44pp.

Date: 'This Day was published' (DJ 24/12/98 p. 3 col. 1)
Authorship: Charles Kerr, whose name appears on the title-page of an identical text, a so-called second edition.

BLACK 2108   TCD: V h 22 no. 10 • RIA: HP 767/ 5 • NLI: P 221/4
BL: 1509/523 (6)

S48 Strictures upon the union between Great Britain and Ireland. Second edition. By Captain Charles Kerr. Dublin: printed for B. Dornin, 1799. 46pp.

Note: This is textually and typographically identical to RIA: HP 767/5, with only t-p alterations for the second, signed, issue – see p. 3 line 7 where property should read propriety, and p. 9 line 4 where agriculture should read agricultural, these uncorrected in either edition. The author seems to have belonged to the Roxbughshire Lt. Dragoons.

BLACK 2014   TCD: Lecky A 4 33 no. 7 • RIA: HP 767/ 6
RIA: HT 327/10 • NLI: P 612/10 • BL: 8145 de 11 (2)

S49 The substance of Mr William Smith's speech on the subject of a legislative union between this country and Great Britain delivered in the House of Commons on Thursday January 24th 1799. A new edition. [London:] Dublin printed; London re-printed for J Wright, 1800. 120pp. (incl ads.)

Authorship: William Cusack Smith - title-page.

RLM: PA 1130/1 • CUL: Hib. 5. 798. 1/4
CUL: Hib. 5. 800. 72 • CUL: Hib. 5. 800. 73

S50 The substance of Mr William Smith's speech on the subject of a legislative union between this country and Great Britain delivered in the House of Commons on Thursday January 24th 1799, and now reduced to the form of an address to the people of Ireland. Dublin: printed and sold by Marchbank, 104pp.

Date: date line (p. 103) February 1st 1799; 'This Day is published' (DJ 7/2/99 p. 3 col 2).
Authorship: William Cusack Smith - title-page.

BLACK 2165   RIA: HT 318/11 • NLI: P 221/16

second edition. Dublin: printed and sold by Marchbank, 1799. 104pp.

RIA: HT 318/12 • RIA: HT 320/3 • RIA: HT 325/3
BL: 1103 g 10 (3) • Bod: Vet A5 e 5669

third edition. Dublin: printed and sold by Marchbank, 1799. 104pp.

TCD: OLS 187 r 6 (6) • RIA: HT 315/1 • RIA: HT 325/9

fourth edition. Dublin: printed and sold by Marchbank, 1799. 104pp.

> TCD: V h 25 no. 11 • RIA: HT 319/13 • CUL: Hib. 5. 799. 95
> CUL: Hib. 7. 799. 45

fifth edition. Dublin: printed and sold by Marchbank, 1799. 104pp.

Note: 'About forty of the fifth, or Large Edition only remains' (DJ 9/3/99 p. 2 col. 1)

> RIA: HP 787/12

sixth edition corrected with additional notes. Dublin: printed and sold by Marchbank, 1799. 56pp.

Date: 'was this Day Published' (DJ 9/3/99 p. 2 col. 1)

> TCD: Crofton 207/1

London: from the Dublin edition, 1799. 106pp.

> BL: 108 a 22

S51 Substance of the speech of Lord Auckland in the House of Peers, April 11 1799, on the proposed address to his majesty respecting the resolutions adopted by the two houses of parliament as the basis of an union between Great Britain and Ireland. London: printed for J Wright, 1799. 54pp. + folding tables.

Date: advertised DJ 25/5/99 p. 2 col 1.
Authorship: - William Eden (1744-1814) 1st baron Auckland - title-page.
Note: RLM: PA 874/5 bears owner's inscription 'from Lord Auckland'.

BLACK 2047

> RIA: HP 788/8 • NLI: P 607/4 (untrimmed)
> RLM: PA 874/5 • BL: 709 (5) • BL: 111 d 56
> Bod: Vet A5 e 460/5 • CUL: Hib. 5. 799. 9
> CUL: Hib. 5. 799. 8 (untrimmed)

second edition. London: printed for J Wright, 1799. 54pp. + folding plates.

> RIA: HT 315/2 • NLI: P 156/3 • BL: 117 h 23

Dublin: printed for J Milliken, 1799. 54pp. + folding plates.

Date: advertised DJ 30/4/99 p 3 col 1.

> TCD: Crofton 212/6 (original state) • TCD: Lecky A 4 36 (4)
> NLI: P 212/4 • NLI: P 607/5 (untrimmed)
> NLI: JP 4857 • RIA: HT 311/11 • BL: 1104 c 25 (6)
> Bod: Vet A5 e 5567/6

third edition. Dublin: printed for J Milliken, 1800. 32pp. + folding tables.

> RIA: HT 336/17

third edition [same imprint] 54, [4]pp.

NLI: I 6551 (1800) Dublin

Cork: printed by George Cherry for the proprietors at the advertising-office, 1799. c 50pp. + folding plates (distinct from other settings.)

NLI: I 6551 Cork 1799

S52 Substance of the speech of the right honourable the earl Temple in the House of Commons on Thursday the 14th February 1799 on the question of the bringing up the resolutions respecting the Irish union, passed in the committee. London: [n.p.], 1799. 52pp.

Authorship: Richard Temple Nugent Brydges Chandos Grenville (1776-1839) – title-page.

RIA: HT 324/2

S53 Substance of the speech of the right hon. Henry Dundas in the House of Commons, Thursday Feb. 7 1799, on the subject of the legislative union with Ireland. Dublin: printed by John Exshaw, 1799. 68pp.

Date: CUL copy of the third London ed. has ms. add. of 'Feb 19' to imprint-date.
Authorship: Henry Dundas (title-page), 1st viscount Melville.

BLACK 2124   RIA: HT 317/8 • RIA: HT 324/3 • RIA: HT 332/3
                 NLI: P 212/3 • BL: 1104 c 25 (3) • BL: 1103 g 7 (2)
                                          Bod: Vet A5 e 5567/6

London: printed for J Wright, [1799]. 68pp.

       RIA: HT 332/11 • Bod: Vet A5 e 460/5 • CUL: Hib. 5. 799. 59
                     CUL: 5. 799. 60 • CUL: Hib. 7. 799. 25

second edition. London: printed for J Wright, [1799]. 68pp.

BL: 8145 b 33

third edition. London: printed for J Wright, [1799]. 68pp.

       RIA: HT 324/1 • NLI: P 610/4 (with half-title of 2nd ed. at back)
                 BL: 111 d 55 • BL: 117 h 19 • CUL: Hib. 5. 799. 61

fourth edition. London: printed for J Wright, [1799]. 68pp.

          RIA: HP 788/ 4 (copy of John Hamilton?) • RLM: PA 875/2
              BL: 08139 ccc 48 (3) • Bod: G pamphlets 2758/10

S54 Substance of the speech of the right honourable Henry Addington, speaker of the House of Commons on the 12th of February 1799 in the committee of the whole house to whom his majesty's most gracious message of the 22d January relative to Ireland was referred. Dublin: printed for J Milliken, 1799. 36pp.

Date: 'This Day published' (DJ 11/4/99 p 1 col 2)
Authorship: Henry Addington (1757-1844, 1st viscount Sidmouth) - title-page.

RIA: HT 322/5
NLI: P 607/1 • RLM: PA 875/4

third edition. Dublin: printed for J Milliken, 1799. 32pp.

TCD: Crofton 207/5 • RIA: HP 788/ 5 • RIA: HT 322/6
NLI: I 6551 (Dublin) 1799 (26) • BL: 1103 g 10 (5)
BL: 1104 c 25 (4) • CUL: Hib. 7. 799. 44

London: printed for J Wright, 1799. 44pp.

CUL: Hib. 5. 799.91

second edition. London: printed for J Wright, 1799. 44pp.

NLI: P 607/2

third edition. London: printed for J Wright, 1799. 44pp.

RIA: HT 322/9 • CUL: Hib. 5. 799. 93

S55 Substance of the speech of the right honourable Lord Sheffield, Monday
April 22 17 [space] 99, upon the subject of union with Ireland. London: printed
for J Debrett, [n.d.] 64pp.

Authorship: John Baker-Holroyd, earl of Sheffield - title-page.

BLACK 2158   RIA: HP 788/ 6 (Presentation copy from Sheffield to Rt. Hon.
Sackville Hamilton.) • RIA: HT 324/4 (first item) • NLI: P 155/5
BL: B 709 (9) • BL: 117 h 28 • BL: 111 d 60
CUL: Hib. 5. 799. 90 • CUL: Hib. 7. 799. 43

printed from a copy corrected by his lordship. Dublin: printed for J Milliken,
1799. 40pp.

RIA: HT 325/7 • RLM: PA 874/4 • BL: 1104 c 25 (8) • BL: 1103 g 10(7)

Dublin: printed by John Exshaw, 1799. 62pp.

Date: 'This Day is published' (DJ 21/5/99 p. 3 col. 1).

TCD: Lecky A 4 36 (5) • RIA: HT 325/6 • NLI: P 153/3
BL: 8145 d 40 • Bod: Vet A5 e 6145/4 • CUL: Hib. 7. 799. 42

S56 Substance of the speech of Robert Peel, esquire, in the House of Commons,
on Thursday the 14th of February 1799, on the question for receiving the report
of the committee on the resolutions respecting an incorporate union with Ireland;
with a correct copy of theresolutions as they were finally amended by the House
of Commons. Dublin: printed by John Exshaw, 1799. 24pp.

Date: 'This Day is Published' (DJ 9/3/99 p. 4 col. 2).
Authorship: Robert Peel (1750-1830) 1st baronet - title-page.

BLACK 2136   TCD: Crofton 212/5 (original state) • RIA: HT 322/4
                              NL: I 6551 (Dublin) 1799 (25) • BL: 1104 c 25 (5)
                                                            RIA: HT 331/3

London: printed for John Stockdale, 1799. 24pp.

                              NLI: P 156/4 • RLM: PA 875/5 (lacks ads.)
                              BL: 117 h 21 (pp. 23-24 adverts.)

S57 Substance of the speeches of the right honourable William Pitt on the 23d
and 31st of January 1799, including a correct copy of the plan, with the debate
which took place in the House of Commons on the proposal for an union between
Great Britain and Ireland, to which are annexed the celebrated speeches of the
right honourable John Foster, late chancellor of the exchequer, now speaker of
the House of Commons of Ireland, on the 12th and 15th days of August 1785
upon the commercial propositions. Dublin: printed by John Exshaw, 1799. 48pp.

Authorship: William Pitt (1759-1806) and John Foster (1740-1848) - title-page.

BLACK 2140   TCD: Lecky A 4 36 (2) • RIA: HP 787/ 18
                    RIA: HT 322/8 • BL: 8135 aa 31 • CUL: Hib. 5. 799. 87

Dublin: printed for J Milliken, 1799. 40pp.

Note: In the early issues the name is given as Fostfr: later issues correct the error.

                                                            BL: 8135 aa 31

London: printed for John Stockdale, 1799. 52pp.

                    BL: 8145 e 64 • Bod: G Pamphlets 1206/1 (cropped)

S58 The substance of three speeches delivered in the House of Commons of
Ireland February 6, March 4, and March 21, 1800 upon the subject of an union
with Great Britain. By R. L. Edgeworth. London: printed for J Johnson by J
Crowder, 1800. 48pp.

Authorship: Richard Lovell Edgeworth (1744-1817) - title-page.

          RIA: HT 336/15 • NLI: P 610/5 (untrimmed) • BL: 1509/693

                                T

T1 Tempora mutantur, or reasons for thinking that it is inconsistent with the
welfare of this kingdom to persist in withholding from the Roman Catholics the
political power, offices and honors exclusively enjoyed by protestants, and that

the admission of the Roman Catholics to a suitable participation of these would not render them predominant in the political system nor consequently be followed by those pernicious effects which are generally apprehended. Dublin: printed by J Moore, 1799. 10pp.

RIA: HT 313/5 • BL: 8146 f 34 (17)

T2 {Unheaded text, commencing} That in order to promote and secure the essential interests of Great Britain and Ireland ... [no imprint, 1799?] 4pp.

BL: 1865 c 9 (64) • Bod: G Pamphlets 2201/30 • Bod: Vet A 5 c 130/11

T3 This present evening Tuesday the 22d January will be represented at the Royal Circus, Foster-Place, a dramatic olio called The union or Ierne divided. The principal characters by a variety of old and new performers collected for the occasion as will be hereafter notified and detailed... [Dublin, 1799] single sheet

TCD: Lecky A 7 38 (item 3 unnumbered)

T4 Thoughts on the constitutional rights of parliament respecting the power of surrendering the legislative independence of Ireland. By A——N——nd. Dublin: printed by V Dowling, 1798. 12pp.

Note: p. 11 'to be continued'.

RIA: HT 306/2 • NLI: P 2/7 • BL: 8145 de 8 (4)

T5 Thoughts on national independence suggested by Mr Pitt's speeches on the Irish union addressed to the people of Great Britain and Ireland. By a member of the honourable society of Lincoln's Inn. [n. pl.:] printed for the author, [1799.] 82pp.

Note: ESTC regards this as textually close to Considerations on national ... (C18 above.) The drop title of the present item reads 'Considerations etc.'

Bod: G Pamphlets 197/5

T6 Thoughts on the projected union between Great Britain and Ireland. Dublin: printed for J Moore, 1797. 48pp.

Authorship: NLI attributes this to Valentine Lawless, (1773-1853 Lord Cloncurry).

BLACK 1988   RIA: HP 732/8 • RIA: HT 302/14 • NLI: Ir 94107 p 14 (6) (untrimmed) • NLI: P 620/7 (untrimmed) • NLI: P 620/6

T7 Thoughts on the times relative to the establishment of Ireland in peace and prosperity by a small reform in her legislation and police; or, on failure of that, how a union with Great-Britain may be best effected to accomplish those desirable ends. By an Irish patriot. Cork: printed by M Harris, 1799. 22pp.16pp.

RLM: PA 35/11 • NLI: I 6551 Cork 1799 (11)
NLI: P 622/11 (lacks pp. 17-22)

T8 Thoughts on an union. By Joshua Spencer. Dublin: printed for William Jones, 1798. 36pp.

Date: CH's ms note on the t-p of RIA: HP 766/2 states 'first edition was published Saturday 1 Decr 1798'.
Authorship: Joshua Spencer - title-page.

BLACK 2031   TCD: Crofton 129/7 • RIA: HT 306/8 • BL: 8145 d 71

second edition. Dublin: printed for William Jones, 1798. 36pp.

                              RIA: HP 766/2 • RIA: HT 308/1 • NLI: P 112/7

second edition. Dublin [n.p.], 1798. 24pp.

                                                        RLM: PA 1045/1

third edition. Dublin: printed for William Jones, 1798. 36pp.

                                        RIA: HT 308/3 • BL: 8145 cc 99

fourth edition. Dublin: printed for William Jones, 1798. 36pp.

            TCD: V h 21 no. 2 • TCD: Crofton 182/2 • TCD: Crofton 202/2
            TCD: Lecky A 4 32 no. 2 • RIA: HT 307/13 • RIA: HT 305/7
            (t-p mutilated) • NLI: P 2/1 • NLI: P 221/5 • NLI: P 251/2
                                            Bod: G pamphlets 1965/6

Cork: printed and sold by J Connor, T White, A Edwards, J Haly, and M Harris, 1798. 24pp.

                                        NLI: I 6551 Cork 1798
                              Univ. of Minnesota (Wilson & Bell Libr) : 941. 57Z

new edition. London: re-printed for John Stockdale, 1798. 32pp.

        RLM: PA 1128/4 • BL: 117 h 11 • BL: 111 d 47 • CUL: Hib. 5. 798. 55
            CUL: Hib. 798. 56 • CUL: Hib. 7. 798. 18 • CUL: Hib. 7. 798. 19

T9 Three letters to a noble lord on the projected legislative union of Great Britain and Ireland. By a nobleman. London: printed by G Sidney for J Wright and J Richardson, 1799. 60pp.

BLACK 2172   BL: 117 h 22 • BL: 111 e 3 • CUL: Hib. 5. 798. 3/8

T10 Tit for tat, or the reviewer reviewed, being an examination of Mr Smith's Review of the Speech of the right hon. John Foster, in a letter addressed to him. By an old correspondent. Dublin: printed by James Moore, 1799. 40pp.

Authorship: attributed to Charles Kendal Bushe (1767-1843), by Black without citing evidence.

BLACK 2056   TCD: Crofton 206/6 • RIA: HT 314/3 • NLI: P 623/4
NLI: I 6551 Dublin (1799) 12 • CUL: Hib. 5. 799. 161

T11 To be or not to be, a nation: that is the question? Dublin: printed by Joseph Mehain, 1799. 32pp.

Date: 'The first pamphlet of the new year' according to an advertisement in DJ 5/1/99 p. 3 col. 1, 'this Day published'.

BLACK 2174   TCD: V h 24 no. 6 • TCD: Lecky A 4 33 no. 13
TCD: Crofton 203/12 • RIA: HP 767/ 20 • RIA: HT 318/4
RIA: HT 328/5 • NLI: P 620/8 • BL: 8145 de 11 (1)

[T12 - number deleted]

T13 To the people of Ireland. [no title page or imprint.] 16pp.

Note: signs off p. 13, Atticus. half-title-page carries ms note 'May 1800'.

RIA: HT 334/12

T14 To the people of Ireland. You are called upon to decide on one of the most momentous questions that ever was agitated in any counry, 'that of an union with another nation' [Dublin, 1800?] single sheet.

Public Record Office (London): H.O. 100/93 [341]

T15 Tracts on the subject of a legislative union, viz. I Letters to Mr Saurin and Mr Jebb; II Speech on a legislative union; III Review of the speech of the right hon. John Foster, Speaker of the House of Commons; IV Letter to Henry Grattan esq MP with animadversions on the speeches of Mr Saurin and Mr Bushe. By William Smith. Dublin: sold by Marchbank and Milliken, 1800. 80, 56, 64, 96pp.

Authorship: William Cusack Smith (1766-1836) - title- page.
Note: This is a composite re-publication of four earlier pamphlets, with a new title-page. Item 2 is a copy of 'the sixth edition corrected with additional notes' of *The substance...* , complete with the Advertisement before the first page of text this latter with drop-head reading *An addresss* etc. Item 3 is 'the third edition; Item 4 is 'the third edition'.

Goldsmiths Collect. 1800 (ser. no. 17,865)

U

U1 Unconnected hints and loose ideas upon the union with two propositions. By a mimber [sic]. Dublin: printed and sold by Marchbank, also by Gilbert, Milliken, and Fine, 1799. 34pp.

Date: 'This Day was published' (DJ 8/1/99 p. 2 col. 4).
Authorship: title-page mottoes include quotations from Walton's Angler and Swift re. Roach, strongly suggesting Sir Boyle Roche as author, perhaps too strongly to be taken at face value.

BLACK 2178   TCD: V h 24 no. 18 • TCD: Lecky A 4 33 no. 14
                            TCD: Crofton 203/9 • RIA: HT 331/15
                     NLI: I 6551 Dublin (1799) 4 • NLI: P 623/3

U2 The union, composed from the favorite [sic] air of God save the king. By Nathaniel Gow. Edinburgh: printed and sold by Gow and Shepherd, [watermarked 1801]. 4p.

Authorship: Nathaniel Gow - title-page.

Note: music only.

                                                  BL: Grenville 442 f (9)
U3 Union 'Our gracious king ...' [a ballad, no imprint, c. 1799] 8pp.

                                                       NLI: P 107/11

U4 The union, a lyric canto appointed to be sung or said in all meeting-houses. [Dublin: Dowling, 1798.] single sheet.

Date: advertised in DJ 15/12/98.

       TCD: S ee 55 (10) • BL: 1325 g 15 (8) • CUL: Hib. oo. 800. 2

U5 The union magazine and imperial register. No. 1 [London:], 1801.

Date: Jan 31 1801 (date-line of postscript p. 77 of no. 1).
Note: 4 vols pub. 1801-2.

          Bod: Per. 3974 e 341/8 • NLI: P 107/14 (No. 1 only)

U6 Union necessary to security addressed to the loyal inhabitants of Ireland. By an independent observer. Dublin: printed for J Archer, 1800. 106pp.

Authorship: Archibald Redfoord, given as author on a Dublin second edition title-page.

BLACK 2259   TCD: Crofton 208/1 • RIA: HT 340/2
                            BL: 8145 dd 73 • CUL: Hib. 5. 800. 66

By Archibald Redfoord. second edition. Dublin: printed for J Archer, 1800. 106pp.

                     RIA: HT 340/1 • RIA: HT 340/3 • NLI: P 125/3
                            BL: o 1609/510 • CUL: Hib. 5. 800. 67

U7 An union neither necessary or [sic] expedient for Ireland, being an answer to the author of Arguments for and against an union between Great Britain and Ireland, considered. By Charles Ball. Dublin: printed by William Porter, 1798. 54pp.

Date: Date line, p. 54, Dec 8th 1798; T-p ms notes in RIA: HP 766/9 read 'published on 10th December 1798' and '10 Decr 1798'.)
Authorship: Charles Ball (title-page).

BLACK 1994   TCD: V h 21 no. 7 • RIA: HP 766/ 9 • RIA: HT 305/9
                         RIA: HT 307/6 • NLI: P 607/6 (untrimmed)
                              NLI: JP 3357 • BL: 8145 dd 2

second edition. By Charles Ball. Dublin: printed by William Porter, 1798. 54pp.

   TCD: Crofton 182/7 • RIA: HT 306/7 • NLI: P 211/1 • NLI: P 251/10
      NLI: P 607/8 • BL: 1509/523 (2) • Bod: G pamphlets 1965/4

third edition. By Charles Ball. Dublin: printed by William Porter, 1799. 54pp.

Note: in the title or has been replaced by nor.

BLACK 2048   TCD: Lecky A 4 32 no. 10 • RIA: HT 330/8

U8 Union or not? By an Orangeman. Dublin: printed by J Milliken, 1799. 42pp.

Date: Date-line, p. 42, December 22nd 1798; 'will be published in the ensuing week' (DJ 22/12/98 p. 3 col. 1).
Authorship: attributed to Harding Giffard, without evidence by Black.

BLACK 2092   TCD: V h 22 no. 13 • TCD: Lecky A 4 33 no. 5
            TCD: Crofton 203/11 • RIA: HP 767/ 10 • RIA: HT 317/14
               RIA: HT 331/18 • NLI: P 221/11 • NLI: P 623/12
                    NLI: JP 4853 • CUL: Hib. 5. 799. 103

U9 Union or separation; of two evils, chuse the least. By R F. Dublin: printed for Bernard Dornin, 1798. 40pp.

Date: 'on Wednesday morning [ie on 26/12/98] will be published' (DJ 24/12/98 p. 3 col. 1); 'this day is published' (DJ 27/12/98 p. 1 col. 3)

BLACK 2034   TCD: V h 22 no. 11 • RIA: HP 767/ 7 • RIA: HT 304/7
                              CUL: Hib. 5. 798. 64

U10 Union or separation; written some years since by the rev. Dr Tucker, dean of Gloucester and now first published in this tract upon the same subject. By the rev. Dr Clarke. London: sold by J Hatchard & J Wright [et al], 1799. 84pp.

Date: 'This Day Published' by J. Milliken (DJ 8/6/99 p. 3 col. 4); no copy of Milliken's imprint of this title has been found.
Authorship: Thomas Brooke Clarke, though CUL credits William Brooke Clarke with editing this item.

BLACK 2177   TCD: 48 g 149 (1) • RIA: HT 332/20
   Bod: G Pamphlets 1965/8 • Bod: G Pamphlets 1206/3 • Bod: 8 B 323/6 Th.

second edition. London: sold by J Hatchard & J Wright [et al.], 1799. 84pp.

RIA: HT 319/2 • CUL: Hib. 5. 799. 102

third edition. With an appendix on the political, commercial & civil state of Ireland. London: sold by J Hatchard [et al], 1799. 866pp. (inc. ads)

CUL: Hib. 5. 798. 2/1 • CUL: Hib. 7. 799.5 (appendix only, as issued?)

U11 Union pamphlets. The following new pamphlets are published this day by Milliken 32 Grafton-Street. [Dublin: Milliken, 1799.] 4pp.

BL: 1509/1173 (2)

U12 Union a plague, in answer to counsellors M'Kenna's Memoire on the projected union. By P Sheehy. Dublin: printed by J Hill, 1799. 52pp.

Authorship: P Sheehy - title-page.

BLACK 2157   TCD: V h 24 (2) • RIA: HT 332/6 (errata on p. [52])
                    NLI: P 212/11 (errata p. 52) • BL: 8146 bbb 23 (2)

U13 Union, prosperity and aggrandizement. London: printed by J W Myers for West and Hughes [et al.], 1800. 88pp.

BLACK 2284   RIA: HT 337/7 • NLI: P 620/9

U14 The union song-book of Great Britain and Ireland. [With appendix]. London: 1801.

Bod: Harding C 3039 • Bod: Harding C 3040

U15 An union to be subjection proved from Mr C's own words in his Arguments for an against; in two parts; part I. By an Irish logician. Dublin: printed for J Rice, 1799. 40pp.

Note: 'to be continued' p. 40.

BLACK 2179   TCD: V h 23 no. 11 • TCD: Crofton 184/5
                 TCD: Crofton 204/5 • TCD: Lecky A 4 34 no. 5
        TCD: 91 p 38 no. 4 • RIA: HT 310/21 • RIA: HT 317/6
              RIA: HT 328/4 • NLI: I 6551 Dublin (1799) 3
              BL: 8145 de 9 (7) • CUL: Hib. 5. 799. 173

U16 The union volunteers; march, troop & quick-step composed & [sic] arranged for the piano forte or harp. By William Shield. London: printed & [sic] sold for the author by T Preston [1800?] 4pp.

Authorship: William Shield - title-page.

BL: Granville 272 q (32)

U17 The union, written & [sic] composed by Mr Dibdin and sung by him in his new entertainment called The cake house. London: printed & [sic] sold by the author, [1800.] 4pp.

Authorship: Charles Dibdin (1745-1814) - title-page.
3 stanzas.

BL: Grenville 380 (14)

U18 Unite or fall. Dublin: printed for J Milliken, 1798. 16pp.

Authorship: Frederick Howard, 1748-1825, earl of Carlisle; so attributed by Bod.

NLI: JP 4855

second edition. Dublin: printed for J Milliken, 1798. 16pp.

Univ. of California (Los Angeles): S/k 1800 1798 C194 u

third edition. Dublin: printed for J Milliken, 1798. 16pp.

New York Public Library: XKF 1798

fifth edition. Dublin: printed for J Milliken, 1798. 16pp.

BL: 8140 df 34

eighth edition. Dublin: printed for J Milliken, 1798. 16pp.

Henry E. Huntinton Library: 326415

London: printed for J Wright, 1798. 24pp.

Univ. of Missouri. Ellis Library: R one DC220.C37. 1798

fifteenth edition. London: printed for J Wright, 1798. 24pp.

Bod: G Pamphlets 1204/3

U19 The utility of union illustrated and set forth in a variety of statements extracted from the works of the most eminent patriots and constitutional writers from the time of James the first to the year 1785 inclusive, interspersed with occasional remarks by the author in a letter to his exellency the marquis Cornwallis. By Theophilus Swift. Dublin: printed by Robert Marchbank for J Milliken, 1800. 70pp.
(Signs off, June 5 1800, p. 69)

Authorship: Theophilus Swift (1746-1815) - title-page.

TCD: Crofton 210/2 • RIA: HT 337/2 • RIA: HT 337/11

V

V1 The vaticination as you will find it written in the 110th no. of Pue's Occurrences, redivivus! the fifth year of the incorporation. Dublin: printed by H Fitzpatrick, 1799. 16pp.

Date: 'This Day is Published' (DJ 22/12/98 p. 3 col. 1); RIA: HT 331/7 top blue cover has ms note 'published 20th Decr 1798'; RIA: HP 767/ 14 , t-p owner-inscription dated 'Decr 26th 1798'.

BLACK 2181   TCD: V h 22 no. 16 • TCD: Lecky A 4 33 no. 10
             TCD: 91 p 38 no. 6 • RIA: HP 767/ 14 • RIA: HT 331/7
                         NLI: P 221/12 • NLI: P 618/2

V2 Verbum sapienti; or a few reasons for thinking that it is imprudent to oppose and difficult to prevent the projected union. Dublin: printed for J Milliken, 1799. 14pp.

Date: date-line (p. 14) 22d December 1798
Authorship: half-title of RLM: PA 868/2 bears ms annotation 'McKenna supposed' - ie Theobald M'Kenna.
BLACK 2183   TCD: V h 22 no. 1 • TCD: 91 p 38 no. 5 • RIA: HT 331/6
      RLM: PA 868/2 • BL: 8145 de 12 (5) • Bod: G Pamphlets 1966/9*

See also NLI: JP 4854, which lacks 11 as a number in pagination sequence and thus ends p. 15 (verso). See also RIA: HP 767/11 for 8pp of printed text [proofs?] irregularly numbered, concluding on a verso 15.

second edition. Dublin: printed for J Milliken, 1799. 16pp.

      TCD: Lecky A 4 33 no. 8 • TCD: Crofton 203/6 • NLI: P 623/7

V3 The vocal miscellany of Great Britain and Ireland, or union song-book comprising two hundred and sixty four of the most approved Scots, Irish, and English songs, with a variety of airs, catches and glees. Berwick: printed for W Phorson and sold in Edinburgh by Mundell, 1797. 360pp.

                                        Bod: Harding C 3113

W

W1 We are favoured with the following copy of a letter written by Mr [Jonah] Barrington to Captain [William] Saurin on resigning his commission in the lawyers' cavalry. [no imprint, dated Jan 20 1799.] single sheet.

Authorship: Sir Jonah Barrington (1760-1834) - text.

                          TCD: Lecky A 7 38 (item 2 unnumbered)

W2 The wedding and bedding, or John Bull and his bride fast asleep, a satirical poem containing an history of the happy pair from their infancy to the present period, with reasons for and means used to accomplish their union; also The matchmakers matched, with their rueful lamentation for the loss of the bride-cake! By T Canning. [London:] printed by Sidney and Evans for J S Jordan, sold also by the author, No. 10 Essex Street, Strand, [no date.] 56pp.

Authorship: T Canning - title-page.
Note: in verse.

RIA: HT 344/14 • RLM: PA 561/11 • BL: 1165 ff 10 (1)

(This item concludes, p. 55, 'end of part the first', and an 'interlude' follows on p. 56: one leaf of ads. added. The title page of the RIA copy bears the neat, uncial inscription R L Edgeworth in the top right hand corner, possibly in the same hand which has numbered the item '213' top centre.) John Foster possessed a copy, now in the library of Queens University Belfast (Foster Coll. 250 iv). Note: Peter Pindar later used the 'wedding and bedding' title re. Queen Charlotte in 1816.

W3 Who's to blame? A new ballad on the union. Air 'The night before Larry was stretched' [Dublin:] published at Dowling's, [1799] single sheet.

TCD: S ee 55 (12) • BL: 1325 g 15 (6) • CUL: Hib. oo. 800. 4

Some Addenda and Untraced Titles

A project for the settlement of Ireland without a union. By a decided friend to the true interests of the British empire. To be had of all the booksellers. Advertised in DJ 7/2/99 (p. 1 col 1) and 12/2/99 (p. 4 col 1) See P22 for a published title close to this.

To the gentlemen who opposed a legislative union with Great Britain. By Verax. [Dublin:] M'Kenzie printer, [1800] single sheet.

Union before subjection to a banditti of robbers, organized for extermination and plunder. This day was published by all the booksellers. (DJ 26/1/99 p. 1 col 2) [Evidently intended to deal with an attack on Joseph Mehain's premises, 22 Castle-street, Dublin on 22 January 1799.]

GENERAL INDEX
(of the introduction and selected notes, by page number)

EVIDENCE RELATING TO AUTHORSHIP
(reference by serial number)

Abbot, Thomas, E3 (part of)
Addington, Henry, S54
Anderson, John, E3 (part of)
Auckland, Lord, *see* Eden, William

Baker-Holroyd, John (Lord Sheffield), S55
Ball, Charles, R22, U7
Barnes, George, R31
Barrington, Sir Jonah, W1
Battier, Henrietta, A6
Beaufort, Daniel, P15 (as editor)
Bentley, Thomas Richard, C20
Beresford, John, O8?, R11?, S24, S25
Bertie, Willoughby (earl of Abington), C24
Bethel, Isaac Burke, R6
Bingley, William, E4, E5
Binns, George, E3 (part of)
Bisset, James, P5
Blair, Thomas, E3 (part of)
Bousfield, Benjamin, L5
Boustead, –, E1?, L9?
Brown, Arthur, R5
Bruce, John, R24 (as compiler)
Burrowes, Peter, M4?
Burrowes, Robert, M4?
Bushe, Charles Kendal, C11, C12, L26, T10

Canning, T., W2
Carey, Charles John, C17
Carleton, Hugh, S35
Carlisle, Earl of, *see* Howard, Frederick
Cawthorne, Joseph, H1, M2
Clarke, Thomas Brooke, D1 (as editor), D7, M9, P9, U10 (as editor)
Cloncurry, Lord, *see* Lawless, Valentine
Collis, John, A10

Cooke, Edward, A24, A25, R29
Coote, Charles, M3
Corbett, William, P8
Cottingham, James Henry, S8
Crosthwaite, Leland, E3 (part of)
Cupples, S., P13

Defoe, Daniel, E8, H8
Dibdin, Charles, U17
Dickey, James, E3 (part of)
Dickinson, Daniel, E3 (part of)
Dillon, Sir John Joseph, L2
Dobbs, Francis, M7, M12
Dodd, James Solas, C1
Douglas, Sylvester, S38
Dowling, Vincent, P18 (as editor?)
Downes, Joseph, O9?
Drennan, William, L22, P27, S2
Duffy, John, E3 (part of)
Duigenan, Patrick, F1, S12, S19, S20
Dundas, Henry, S53

E., W., A15
Eden, William (Lord Auckland), S51
Edgeworth, Maria, C3
Edgeworth, R. L., S58
Elliott, Gilbert (Lord Minto), A1, S18

Fitzgibbon, John (earl of Clare), N10, S26
Foster, John, C13, R12 (part of), R20 (part of), R21 (title-page ref. only), S13, S27, S28, S29, S30, S31, S32, S57 (part of)

Galbraith, James, A19
Gay, Nicholas, S46
Geoghegan, Jacob, E3 (part of)
Geraghty, James, C16, P12

PRINCIPAL BOOKSELLERS, PRINTERS, PUBLISHERS ETC.
(place of publication Dublin, unless otherwise stated; reference by serial number)

Advertiser Office (Cork), O4, O8
Anti-Jacobin Press (London), I6, R2

Black, E. (Belfast), O8
Burnside, T., A24, O8

Campbell & Shea, R20
Cherry, G. (Cork), R23, R26, S18, S51
Connor, J. (Cork), A16, C12, F7, L15, M6, N7
Corbet, W., P8

Debrett, J. (London), C2, C12, L4, O3, O10, R9, S16, S27, S29, S42, S55
Doherty & Simms (Belfast), P13
Dornin, B., I2, I3, P14, S22, S47, S48, U9
Dowling, V., H4, L17, L30, N3, O11, O12, O13, P1, P4, P18?, P19, P25, T4, U4, W3

Exshaw, J., B2, C6, C10, E8, H8, S18, S35, S41, S46, S53, S55, S56, S57

Fitzpatrick, H., C3, C23, H6, I5, L2, L3, N7, O10, R7, R26, V1
Folds, W., L6
Folingsby, G., C3, L18, M6, P27, R1, S2

Gilbert, W., R6, R31, U1
Graisberry & Campbell, B2, R23
Grierson, G., A4, A5, S39

Haly, J. (Cork), A16, A18, E3, L5, L9, L15, N7, S27
Harris, M. (Cork), A16, A24, C12, D6, L15, N7, T7
Hatchard, J. (London), C20, L16, M9, P9, P24, R10, U10
Henshall, T., A8, S13
Herald-Office (Cork), L27, S9
Hill, P. (Edinburgh), H9
Hime, B1, N11

Johnson, J. (London), C3, S58
Jones, J., M7
Jones, W., C20, I1, P20, R9, S4, T8

Longman & Rees (London), H9

M'Kenzie, W., O19, P21, S8, T12
Marchbank, R., A14, L13, M3, P15, P23, R28, S50, T15, U1
Mehain, J., P6, S3, T11
Milliken, J., A1, A16, A17, A19, A21, A24, C1, C14, C20, D1, E2, E7, F1, F3, G1, I6, I8, L8, L20, L24, L28, L31, L32, M9, N2, N6, O6, O17, O18, P2, P3, P9, P17, P26, P28, R2, R12, R18, R23, R27, S6, S10, S19, S23, S24, S25, S26, S34, S37, S38, S43, S44, S51, S54, S55, S57, T15, U1, U8, U11, U18, U19, V2
Moore, J., A3, A7, A8, A10, A11, A13, A15, A18, A20, C2, C11, C12, C13, C22, D2, D3, E1, E6, F5, F6, K1, L10, L12, L22, L25, L26, M11, M12, O5, P22, R13, R14, R15, R16, R17, R19, R21, S1, S14, S21, S27, S28, S30, S32, T1, T6, T10

Peppard, R. (Limerick), C19